T0171453

Papa was a Rolling Stone

Fathers of Charleston

Michael A Davis
as told Sarah Barnes

WestBow
PRESS
A DIVISION OF THOMAS NELSON

WestBow Press books may be ordered through booksellers or by contacting:

WestBow Press
A Division of Thomas Nelson
1663 Liberty Drive
Bloomington, IN 47403
www.westbowpress.com
1-(866) 928-1240

Because of the dynamic nature of the Internet, any web addresses or links contained in this book may have changed since publication and may no longer be valid. The views expressed in this work are solely those of the author and do not necessarily reflect the views of the publisher, and the publisher hereby disclaims any responsibility for them.

Any people depicted in stock imagery provided by Thinkstock are models, and such images are being used for illustrative purposes only.

Certain stock imagery © Thinkstock.

ISBN: 978-1-4497-5675-8 (sc)
ISBN: 978-1-4497-5676-5 (hc)
ISBN: 978-1-4497-5674-1 (e)

Library of Congress Control Number: 2012919618

Printed in the United States of America

WestBow Press rev. date: 12/07/2012

Contents

Dedication

This book is dedicated to all my brothers and sisters—those I got to know in this journey of discovery and those who died before my journey began. Getting to know the ones who are left has made me realize how important it is to love and care for each other while we have the opportunity.

I love each and every one of you, and I thank you for being who and what you are.

Acknowledgments

I wish to acknowledge the following people for assisting me in the creation, writing, and publication of this book:

Cynthia Vorhis, my cousin; my wife, Teresa Davis; and my sister Diane Davis Mitter, for their enthusiasm, encouragement, dedication, and wisdom.

Sarah Barnes, my co-writer and editor, for her vision, insight, and editorial skills.

Thank you all so very much.

Preface

What follows is a record of my search for my father, a man I never knew. I am now fifty-three years old and have spent the last three years searching. Initially, all I hoped to do was find out where he was buried.

In the process, I learned much more than that. I discovered some extremely disturbing things about this man. Most particularly, that he was married three times and fathered at least twenty-two children. He did some interesting things and some things that would put him in jail if he did them today.

Papa was a complex man, full of contradictions. A hardworking, talented bricklayer, a musician, an outdoorsman, and a wanderer and philanderer. At times viciously mean, at other times he was a fun-loving prankster.

On this journey of discovery, I learned many things about my father. But mostly I learned about me, about who I am and what I'm made of.

Ultimately, my search for this man I never knew became a life-changing experience.

Prologue

Approaching the cemetery entrance, I glance at my watch: 1:10 p.m. Twenty minutes before I have to leave for the airport. Parking the car in the visitor parking lot, I grab the printout of the cemetery division sections with the plot I had highlighted: D-26. Within minutes, I am standing in front of the gravestone I have been looking for.

Robert Benjamin Davis
1899–1970

A whoosh of air travels from my gut and escapes through my mouth, and I realize I have been holding my breath.

Well, here you are. You son . . . of . . . a . . . bitch. At last. What a way to meet your father, I thought.

Two years of searching culminates here. Today, March XX, 2007, at this gravesite. As I sort through the emotions flooding my heart and mind, I feel my legs start to buckle. I kneel down, raise my left leg, and rest my head with my arm on my left knee.

Why? I thought. *Why did you leave us? I hate you! We needed you. I needed you.*

Moments pass, and the anger gives way to pain as an overwhelming sadness wells up from the pit of my stomach. For a minute, I think I am going to be sick. But the nausea passes, and tears spring from my eyes and spill down my cheeks instead.

"I needed to love you, Pop. I would have forgiven you."

A jumble of images flash through my brain—bits and pieces of the people, places, and things I've seen and heard during the past two years of searching for the answer to who my father was and why he left us.

1

The Early Years
(1899–1926)

In 1899 in Charleston, South Carolina, Papa was born Robert Benjamin Davis, the son of Enoch Nathan Davis and Annie Kent. He lived there and in Adams Run from 1899 through 1921.

When he finally stopped growing, he was tall—6 foot 5 inches—weighed 240 pounds, and had dark hair. As a youngster, he rode his horse to school every day. And he often accompanied his parents when they drove their horse and buggy to the market downtown, a pretty common mode of transportation in those parts of the country in 1910.

He loved the outdoors and went fishing, hunting, and tracking every chance he got. As a teenager, he worked on weekends as a tour guide for hunters and fisherman in and around Charleston Harbor and the surrounding areas.

He could be a jokester and loved to dress up like a cowboy and act like he was from "out West." He loved eating raw oysters right from the shell, a favorite Charlestonian delicacy then and now.

Early on in his adult life, he started working as a carpenter and later learned how to work with concrete, eventually becoming an excellent bricklayer. In Tennessee, when he was married to Mama, much of his work was with Crab Orchard stone and block.

But then there was his mean side. The Bible talks about the "sins of the father." I wonder if my dad was mistreated or molested as a child, and that's why he did some of the cruel things he did later to his own children. Who knows?

God knows, of course, and He will ask my father that very question some day.

One of Papa's brothers, Pete Davis, raised several children. From what I've learned, Pete was a good, Christian man. Throughout their lives, he tried to help my dad get straightened out. He even came to St. Charles, Missouri, when my father died in 1970 and took his body back to be buried with others in the family in the White Church Cemetery in Ravenel, South Carolina.

Now *That's* What You Call a
Handsome Dude!

"Cowboy Roy"
(His Favorite Pose)
Circa 1944

Michael A Davis

Pals – Papa and a Friend

2

The First Twelve

In 1920 Robert Benjamin Davis met and fell in love with his cousin, Virginia Carrow Hodges, who was from Adams Run, South Carolina. They were married on March 16, 1921, in Charleston County, South Carolina. He worked as a carpenter and learned concrete work as a laborer when he was hired to help restore Fort Sumter in Charleston, South Carolina. He also found work as a fishing guide from time to time. When his brother John decided to move to Texas, Papa and Virginia moved too and lived there about a year.

Daytona Beach, Florida, in 1926 was beginning to boom, so they left Texas, and he went to work helping build the hotels and resorts springing up all along the beaches. He even worked on the racetrack there. They lived in Jacksonville and Miami before settling down in Port Orange for good.

Port Orange is just outside Daytona Beach, and there was plenty of work all over the area. In between his union jobs, he managed to find time to build two houses for his own family.

Then there were those times he would just take off—acting, singing, and playing his guitar every night. He became a member of a group called the Florida Ramblers.

Florida Ramblers to Play at Dance Tonight

"Florida Ramblers seven-piece orchestra have contributed they services for the dances being given tonight at the Mira Mar auditorium for the benefit of the unemployment fund being raised by the committee working with the Sarasota County Welfare association.

The dance tonight is the first of a series planned for each Wednesday night to raise funds for the unemployed. Dancing tonight will commence at 9 o'clock.

— Sarasota Herald-Tribune, Jul 1, 1931

— http://news.google.com/newspapers?id=CTshAAAAIBAJ&sji
d=NWQEAAAAIBAJ&pg=1

The name fit him perfectly. With them, he was a jolly, fun-loving guy. At home, not so much. Why his wife allowed him to do this, I don't know. Maybe she didn't know what he was doing or where he was going. Maybe she was just glad to be rid of his volatile disposition for a while. He would just come and go as he pleased; sometimes he would leave and be gone for months.

He was now a member of the bricklayers' union, and that's how he got most of his jobs. So in between jobs, he got into the habit of coming and going whenever and wherever he wanted. It was a habit he followed all the rest of his life. It's how he got away with most of the bad things he did. When he got in trouble, he just picked up and left.

In the twenty years he lived with Virginia in and around Daytona Beach, he fathered twelve children: eight sons and four daughters named Robert B. Jr., Neil Roger, Nadine Lorraine, Frank L., Raymond Conrad, John Lee, Yvonne Theresa, Malcolm C., Zane Mark, Amelia, June M., and Terril.

I got to meet Amelia in 2008, after I learned about my father's first marriage and family. Listening to the stories she told me somehow made me feel as if I'd known them all my life. It was horrible and shocking to learn the way Papa treated them. I just wish in my heart I could have helped them in some way. Of course, I wasn't even born at the time.

Papa was what Amelia called a "hard-core" man. He would make the kids stay out of the house all day until it got dark. Sometimes he would get drunk and beat the kids. I cannot imagine such a thing. But I do believe her. Amelia told me his wife, Virginia, was a strong-willed woman also and ruled her house with an iron fist. It just seems to me my little brothers and sisters didn't stand much of a chance with either their mom or their dad.

Because Amelia is the only one left from this family, I know very little about the others, and most of it is pretty heartbreaking.

Michael A Davis

Bits and Pieces of
Their Lives

Robert B. Davis Jr., the oldest child, was born March 4, 1922. Papa and his wife, Virginia, were living with the Seminole Indians in the Everglades at the time. After a few months, they moved to Charleston, South Carolina. Severe beatings from Papa when he was a young boy caused Robert to have partial vision in his right eye. Still, he managed to join the army in April of 1943, taking his enlistment training at Camp Blanding, Florida.

After military service, he worked at a broom factory in Mississippi. At some point, Robert married, but he was divorced by the time he died of lung cancer on July 16, 1994, in Jackson, Mississippi. He is buried in Woodland Cemetery, Port Orange, Florida.

Neil Roger Davis was born in September 1923 in Charleston, South Carolina, and died in 1936, at twelve years of age. The tragic circumstances of his death are recorded later in Amelia's diary. He is buried in Jacksonville, Florida.

Nadine Lorraine Davis was born in 1925. She married Guy R. Miller, a chiropractor, and they had one son, Neil. After Guy died, she married Max Conyers in Carson City, Nevada, in September 1976.

Nadine worked as an audit supervisor at Sears Roebuck in Salinas, California, for twenty-two years. When she retired in 1978, she returned to her childhood home in Daytona Beach, Florida. When she died in California in 2005, her body was cremated.

Lorraine Davis and son Neal 1954

Michael A Davis

OBITUARY—*The Californian,*
Salinas, CA—11/29/2005

Lorraine Miller Conyers, 1925–2005

Lorraine Miller Conyers, 81, of Port Orange, Fla., a longtime Salinas resident, died Saturday, Nov. 26, 2005, in Port Orange.

She was born July 21, 1925, in Miami, Fla., and grew up in Port Orange. She retired to Port Orange in 1978 after 22 years as an audit supervisor at Sears Roebuck in Salinas. She enjoyed gardening, traveling to Lake Tahoe and to the Arizona desert. She also enjoyed spending time with her family and friends.

She was preceded in death by her first husband, Dr. Guy R. Miller of Salinas, and her second husband, Max Conyers of Salinas and Port Orange.

Memberships: Salinas and Daytona Beach Moose Lodges.

Survivors: son, Neil (Gwen) Miller of Salinas; grandson, Guy E. Miller of San Luis Obispo; brother, Raymond Davis of Florida; sister, Amelia (Jack) Dean of Florida; niece, Mary Ann Mueller of Port Orange; numerous nieces and nephews.

Services: A private family memorial will be held.

Memorials: Hospice of Volusia, Flagler County, 3800 Woodbriar Trail, Port Orange, Fla. 32129.

Arrangements: Struve and Laporte Funeral Chapel.

Information: www.struveand la porte.com.

Originally published November 28, 2005.

Frank L. Davis was born on September 28, 1926, in Miami, Florida. In 1945, when he was just nineteen, he enlisted in the Quartermaster Corps of the US Army and eventually served in the Pacific Theater. His enlistment papers state, "Hawaiian Dept., Regular Arm, Philippine Scout."

When he returned to civilian life, Frank followed in the footsteps of his father and became a construction worker and bricklayer.

My understanding from family members is that Frank married a German woman named Annalese, and they had two children, Virginia and Mary Ann, but he was divorced at the time of his death.

According to his death certificate, he was found on October 14, 1991. Cause of death is listed as "Acute Drug Intoxication." He was sixty-five years old and was living alone in an apartment in Daytona Beach at the time. He is buried in Woodland Cemetery, Port Orange, Florida.

Frank Davis (teenager) 1942

Frank Davis 1952

Frank and naan ramie July 1957

Virginia and Annalist

Raymond Conrad (Cocky) Davis was born on July 17, 1927. He served in the army during World War II.

According to Amelia, he inherited Papa's violent temper. He never married and lived with his mother for many years. He had a standoff with the police in 2002, which resulted in his incarceration in a mental facility in Platkia, Florida. He died there on February 3, 2007.

Raymond is buried in Woodland Cemetery, Port Orange, Florida.

Raymond Conrad Davis 1938

Raymond Conrad Davis 1944

JAN 1958

Raymond Conrad Davis 1958

John Lee Davis was born June 20, 1929, and died December 19, 1985, in Port Orange, Florida. That is all I know about him.

Yvonne Theresa Davis was born March 20, 1930, in Liberty, Texas, where Papa and his first wife, Virginia, were living at the time. She was nicknamed "Honey" because of the lovely olive tone of her skin; she tanned easily.

According to family rumor, Honey left home at a young age and was married several times. She was quite beautiful but contracted lupus in her late twenties. That may be why she was never able to have children of her own.

Her last husband, Harry Lee Walters, adored her. Lee worked as a machinist and welder. When Honey and Lee were living in Lakeland, Florida, they opened their home to wayward girls. Honey had a loving and caring spirit. The girls were rough around the edges, but Honey knew how to handle them; she could be tough if need be. Still, the girls always knew she was there for them.

Honey died in October 1992. She was living in Fort Worth at the time. I could not find her gravesite, but family members say she is buried in Arkansas.

Yvonne Teresa Davis age 10

Yvonne Teresa Davis

Michael A Davis

Honey Davis and Husband Lee Circa 1980

Honey Davis and Husband Lee Walters
Circa 1968

Malcolm Campbell Davis was born February 3, 1932. He, too, joined the army. After leaving the service, he worked in the construction industry. Like his father, he was a "wanderer" and spent several years out West mining for gold. He, too, was partially blind in one eye because of being beaten so severely by our father when he was a child. His condition was diagnosed as tunnel vision. Malcolm never married and died of a heart attack in January of 1979. He was just forty-six years old.

He is buried in Woodland Cemetery, Port Orange, Florida.

Malcolm Campbell Davis 1940

Zane Mark Davis was born on July 28, 1933, in Allendale, Florida. His sight was impaired in one eye as the result of the beatings he received from Papa.

Even so, he joined the army and served in the Korean conflict. His mother, Virginia, had to sign for him to enlist because he was not yet eighteen. He was captured, and when he was recovered by the United States, he was suffering from "shell shock," which affected him for the rest of his life. He never again felt secure, and he found it difficult to leave the house or meet people.

Family members think he may have followed his father into the construction/bricklayer industry after completing his military service. However, in my research for this book, I could find no record of Zane in the *Social Security Death Index*, which suggests to me that if he worked, it must have been very sporadic.

Virginia felt responsible for his disability, and she carried the guilt of her decision to sign his enlistment papers the rest of her life. Zane never married and lived with her until she died. Then he lived with Lorraine.

Zane was sixty-six when he died of severe hypertension and heart disease in 1999. He is buried in Woodland Cemetery, Port Orange, Florida.

Zane Mark Davis 1940

Zane Mark Davis outside Georgia Hospital 1950

Zane Mark Davis in uniform 1952

Zane Davis, 1952

Zane Davis, 1958

Michael A Davis

Amelia Joyce Davis was born May 16, 1935. As a child, she, too, was blinded in one eye by our father. After graduating from Sea Breeze High School in Daytona Beach, Florida, she married John Lunquist in 1951. The marriage was short lived, and by 1952, she was back home. Then in 1956, she met and married Jack Deen. She and Jack raised her two girls from her first marriage, Elizabeth Frances and Virginia Ann. In addition, they had three boys: Jack Jr., Ronald, and Michael.

At some point, they adopted their first grandson, Daniel. He was quite a wonder. He had a photographic memory and did well in school, always getting high honors. He became a nurse but developed Bell's palsy. He died of lung cancer at age thirty-seven.

Daniel knew Amelia had always wanted to go to college, so when he was attending I.T.T., he talked her into going, too. She took classes for five years, studying any and everything she always wanted to know.

Amelia presently lives in Florida. Through the years, she kept a diary and has shared some of her memories from those times with me. With her permission, I have included them later in the book, just as she told them to me.

Amelia Davis and June Davis

June Davis and Amelia Davis

Raymond Davis and Amelia Davis

Amelia and Ginger (daughter) 1952

Amelia, Jack, Ginger 1958

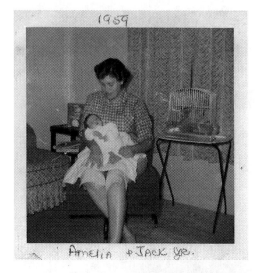

This is a picture of Amelia and Lorraine, Circa 1952

Michael A Davis

My mother, *June Glory Davis*, was born January 8, 1938. She married William Gail Myers in 1955. He was a professional skater and owned and operated a rink in Tampa, Florida. After their marriage, June worked with him managing the rink. In 1972, they moved to Ft. Collins, Colorado, and my dad built Rocky Hill Skating Rink.

Mom had worked as a secretary in an insurance agency before I was born and had beautiful handwriting. She also played the organ beautifully, and I remember her music. She was teaching herself to play the piano shortly before she died. She was a great cook and cooked every holiday dinner except for the last one, Thanksgiving, before she died.

Having parents who owned and operated a skating rink, it is not surprising that my sister and I learned to skate at an early age. If we weren't in school or sleeping, that's where we'd be. In addition to skating, Mom was the consummate homemaker and loved to sew and managed to find time to make all my costumes for my skating competitions. She made my doll clothes and my sister's summer playclothes, too. She loved musicals, and I grew up watching all the old movies: *Camelot, Oklahoma,* etc.

Until we moved to Colorado, she was very close to "Little Granny," as I called her mom, and we would go there once a month or so and help her clean house and take her shopping. My favorite place to stop on the way back was the Steak 'n Shake. Going out to eat back then was a special treat, not a regular thing like today.

When we moved to Colorado, she became even more domestic, learning to make delicious homemade pies (from scratch!) and to can fruits. And then she took up ceramics in her "spare time." To this day, I treasure the two statues she made for me.

My parents divorced in 1976, but Daddy intended to give Mom the rink, so it could be handed down to us girls as a way to ensure we would always have a source of income. Unfortunately, Mom died six months after the divorce without a signed will, and the court made him sell the rink, because I was a minor (and the oldest) of the children.

Mom died on the 28th of November 1976 of a sudden massive cerebral hemorrhage. It was three days after Thanksgiving. She was just thirty-eight. She had suffered severe headaches one week prior to her death. I loved her so and miss her very much.

—Marvel Lynn Myers, December 2011

June Glory Davis 1941

June Davis Myers, unknown, 1954

June Glory Davis 1955

June Davis, unknown 1955

June +mother   1959

June and mother

June Davis and baby Marvel Lynn 16 weeks old

Mother June and Marvel Lynn 1966

Michael A Davis

Mother June and Marvel Lynn 1968

June Myers, Bill Myers, Marcel Lynn 1968

June Davis Myers shortly before she died 1976, Age 38

Terril Leon Davis was born on the October 25, 1939, in Allendale, Florida, and died May 14, 1942.

"His death was a complete and utterly senseless tragedy.

Mama and Daddy were both off working, and Grandma Elizabeth was sick. Lorraine, the oldest then living at home, wasn't home. Honey (Yvonne), herself only twelve, was watching baby Terril. The rest of us kids were there, helping. He kept getting into everything, so we penned him up. We blocked off a square section of the room near where we were washing clothes.

Daddy had filled our kerosene lamps before leaving for work that morning but hadn't tightened the lid on the can, which was sitting on a shelf in the blocked-off area where Terril was playing. Terril picked the can of kerosene clear off the shelf. But when he did, it tipped and spilled kerosene all over his chest and down his back from his neck down.

It was very hot that day, and before Honey came back to check on him, it had dried and turned into a huge blister. He cried all afternoon. When Mama got home and picked him up, the blister broke, and the baby went into convulsions and died."

—Amelia Davis Deen, January 2012

Mother Virginia and Terri

Virginia with Amelia, June and the house that Papa built.

Mother and Frank

Granny Virginia, Missy, Baby Jack Dee Jr.

Grant and friends

Virginia and aunt Ethel 1979

Virginia Dow divas 1979

Michael A Davis

By the time I started this search to find my father, all these brothers and sisters had died except for Amelia. Yet somehow, I feel close to them. Maybe I'm the lucky one, because I never suffered the physical pain this man was so good at inflicting. Instead, I suffered the emotional pain of not having a father.

What I've learned through this is that I would rather have had no father than one who treated me the way my father treated his first family. You might say it was the lesser of two evils.

Papa had a double personality, for sure. When he wasn't drinking, he was hardworking—generous even. He was an expert bricklayer and builder of houses. To those who knew him on the road, he was musically talented and loved laughing, singing, and playing his guitar.

But when he was home and drinking, he became ugly and abusive. And he drank. A lot. It brought out this ugly side, this mean side, and he became a wife and child beater. And worst of all, he became a sexual deviant. This brings us to the how and why of him leaving this family in 1945.

This is what I've been able to piece together from talking with Amelia and others.

They were living on Peninsular Drive in Daytona Beach at the time. Papa raped the grandmother, Virginia's mother, who lived with them. Why? Maybe he was drunk. By then, the boys were almost grown, pretty big, and strong. They decided to put an end to his abusive treatment once and for all. Maybe they beat him up or at least planned to. At any rate, to retaliate, Papa set the house on fire. But first he removed a chest he had built by hand in 1926.

Why he wasn't arrested on the spot, I don't know. Somehow the family recovered and temporarily moved to a rental home. Pretty soon, the police did get involved and came looking for him. He had to leave, and this time it's for good.

"On the lam"[1] from the police, he took off and ended up in Crossville, Tennessee, looking for Crab Orchard stone to build houses. But first he met my mother, Wilma Parsons.

---

[1] According to the *Online Etymological Dictionary*, lam means "flight," as in on the lam, 1897, from a US slang verb meaning "to run off" (1886), of uncertain origin, perhaps somehow from the first element of *lambaste*, which was used in British student slang for "beat" since the 1590s.

3

On the Run
(1945–1960)

Papa left his family for good and didn't stop 'til he got all the way to Crossville, Tennessee, an area famous for its Crab Orchard stone. I guess he rightly figured he could find plenty of work laying bricks and building houses with all that stone just lying around, waiting to be harvested.

But first he met Mama.

By the time Papa met Mama, he was forty-six years old. Mama was twenty-seven and had two small children to care for. Two kids instead of twelve! Maybe he considered that an improvement. At any rate, it didn't discourage him from hooking up with her. He told her he had been in the army for twenty years. I guess she believed him. She was an uneducated farm girl, after all, with a need of her own.

This was in the forties, remember, and a single woman with two children by two different men was a disgraceful thing. So she was looking for a way out of her shameful circumstances. In a way, they were two of a kind. Both had conducted themselves contrary to standards of decency, morality, and integrity.

Papa had left Florida in a full-sized, black truck, ideal for transporting furniture or heavy-duty construction material. Shortly after he and Mama got together in Crossville, he managed to get a load of bricks from the Crab Orchard Stone Mine, and he and Wilma and her two children took off for Murfreesboro, Tennessee. Those bricks helped him get started in the house-building trade again. Papa and Mama stayed there a few months and then got married on September 11, 1945.

Papa was still on the run from the Florida police for raping Virginia's mother back in April of that year. So it wasn't long before he decided to move his new family to Lewisburg, where he thought he would be safer. I guess he figured it would be easy to hide in a small town. They stayed there a couple of months. He even started going to church, but that didn't last long. It just wasn't in his nature, I reckon, or maybe the things he heard in church made him feel too guilty.

Soon he was back to his old ways of leaving for weeks at a time. Where did he go? What did he do? At the time, who knew?

He was building houses again and making good money, so he was providing for his family financially if not otherwise.

"I remember my daddy being gone a lot," my sister Diane recently told me. "But when he came back, he always had gifts for everyone."

Here is a postcard my brother Stanley got from Papa sometime in 1950:

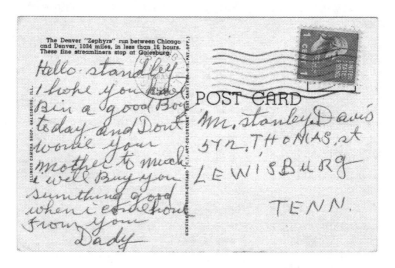

The picture is identified—Famous "Denver Zephyr" and C.B. & Q. R.R. Station, Galesburg, Ill.—and postmarked Galesburg. I wonder what he was doing there.

I now know that some of his absences took him back to Florida. Sometimes it was to visit his musician friends. His Florida Rambler buddies had known him as "Happy Davis," so I can imagine they were happy to see him again. One time he went back to study and record the construction methods he had used on the two houses he had built while living there. He was building houses again in Tennessee and wanted to use similar design and construction methods.

Typical of his nomadic nature, each time he returned to Florida, he made a halfhearted attempt to get back with first wife, Virginia, in Daytona Beach. It never worked, of course, because unlike his musician friends, Virginia was never happy to see him.

If there was one thing Papa was good at, besides leaving, it was building houses. When I finally got to visit the places he lived with his two other families, I could always recognize the houses he built because of their distinctive style.

In 1952, my brother William Roy was born, named after Papa, who always called himself Roy B., not Robert B. By this time, Papa's roaming and his penchant for trouble were once again catching up with him. Even when he stayed home and worked, his drinking brought out his mean and vicious nature. Folks in the neighborhood eventually got wind of his strange behavior.

You see, the kids in the neighborhood hung out at our house a lot, and when Papa wasn't on the road, he enjoyed hanging out with them. Unfortunately, hanging out with the kids frequently resulted in him touching them in inappropriate ways. They told their folks, of course, and some of the parents started to investigate.

Finally, one day they came to our house in Lewisburg, intending to talk to him about the rumors they'd heard. What did Papa do? He put a shotgun in the window and fired both barrels! Luckily he didn't hit anyone.

Now he needed to move again. This time he took his family to Nashville, to an area known as "the Nations," where each street was named after a different state. This neighborhood was near the Tennessee State Prison. I think some of the kids who lived there spent a night or two in juvenile detention. If not, they should have, because almost every street had a group of tough, young kids who formed themselves into street gangs—one gang per street. They would declare the street their nation, and any outside kid would have to get permission to be there and fight to prove it.

So Papa and Mama, ten-year-old Clifford, six-year-old Stanley, and new baby William moved to the house on Delaware Avenue, two miles from the Tennessee State Prison and right next to I-40. The following year, 1953, my sister Wanda Diane was born.

They lived in a large, old, brick home right next to the Tennessee Orphans' Home. Papa would be out every day, building houses there in West Nashville. In 1957, he was working on the Ford Glass Plant, which was being built. Mama liked this, because Clifford, now fifteen, and Stanley, eleven, could frequently work with Papa in the summer.

As usual, from time to time Papa would start drinking and running around. Sometimes he beat Mama. Clifford and Stanley would try to protect her, but that just meant he beat up on all three of them. Nobody ever got the best of Papa in a physical fight.

I was born March 2, 1959, and six months later, my father was nowhere to be found. We didn't know it at the time, but we would never see him again. He left us with no food, no money, and when the weather turned cold, no heat.

So there was my mother, a woman with a ninth-grade education, trying to support five kids under the age of eighteen. To make matters worse, we were living smack-dab in the middle of where I-40 was coming through. We had to move. I mean, we really had to move. The county gave us notice that we had to be out in eighteen months. For some reason, Mama couldn't get motivated to do anything about it. Considering her lack of education, the prospect must have seemed overwhelming. Plus, she thought Papa would be coming back, like he always did. So she just sat there, waiting. When she wasn't working, that is.

We had no family or friends to help us, and our situation was dire. Finally, everyone else had moved from the street. And then, in 1962, the state workers on the I-40 project actually came and set our barn on fire. We were still living in the house, and we had chickens, a donkey, two or three cats, and a couple of dogs. Regulations about having animals within the city were not enforced back then, like they are now. One of our dogs, named Ding Pot, got his back leg stuck in the new highway's pavement while trying to escape. After that, his back leg was useless, and he had to hop around on three legs. (Me and that poor dog had at least one thing in common—we both lost our "paws"!)

So there we were, with Papa basically leaving us there to survive or not, just like he did his first family in Daytona Beach,

Florida. How can a man just walk away from his wife and children? I still don't know the answer to that question.

What I do know is God works in ways I do not understand. We finally got the money from the state of Tennessee so we could move. One month later, that's exactly what we did. On the day we actually moved out, the wrecking crew was coming in the front door, starting their demolition, while we were moving out the back door! Even they knew enough to save the beautiful, old, wooden front door, the Victorian fireplace, and the solid hardwood floors.

We only moved a mile away. With the money from the state, Mama purchased a house on Wyoming Avenue in the community of Sylvan Park. From "the Nations" to Sylvan Park, it was like going from night to day.

So what would become of us now? Would we be taken from our mother? Would we be put in an orphanage?

One good thing about living in the middle of a good neighborhood like Sylvan Park was that we could walk to the store, to school, and to church, and the bus service was close by if we needed it. If we had been someplace more isolated, I don't think we could have made it. Even so, these were really hard times. Mama worked nights at jobs that did not pay much. Mostly it was factory work. One factory was M.E.C., then located on Allied Drive, where they made key chains and novelties. Another was Sanders Manufacturing on Centennial Boulevard in West Nashville; they made pencils and wood products. Another I remember was Kahn's Five and Dime.

Fire stations, then as now, collected toys for disadvantaged children. Sometimes they got toys that were damaged or too worn to give, so they ended up throwing them away. For instance, a doll with only one arm or a stuffed animal missing an ear would be thrown out. Mama was too proud to let us go to the "charity party" given by the fire department, but I do remember going to Fire Station 13 on Charlotte Avenue in West Nashville one Christmas, searching through the throwaway bin, and finding just what I had been wishing for: a cap gun. I was three years old.

Day by day, life went on. Or it doesn't. For us it did, and somehow we managed. Clifford and Stanley, being the oldest, helped care for the rest of us the best they could while Mama worked. But by 1965, they had both moved out. Soon they were married with families of their own to care for.

We needed a dad, and Mama needed a husband.

I look back on those years and wish I could have helped our mother more. At the time, she was just Mama. Now I realize as a woman and a wife, his leaving must have hurt her in ways I never understood at the time.

In 1966 we moved again, this time to 4709 Nebraska Avenue, just a few blocks from the Wyoming house and still in the Sylvan Park community. This was an older home, built in 1927, with three bedrooms. Mama had one bedroom, Diane had another, and we rented out the third bedroom. William slept on the couch in the living room, and I slept on the floor in Mama's room.

Some of our renters were kind of "strange." Mostly they were men, but a few were women. The men worked low-paying construction jobs and spent most of their money and spare time at the local bars. I think you get the picture. They weren't exactly the kind of people you would choose to expose your children to, if you had the choice.

I remember one guy in particular; his name was Tony Perdue. He had a good job at the R. C. Cola plant on Charlotte Avenue and seemed to hang around the house a lot whenever Diane was home. Mama didn't like that one bit, and she kept a watchful eye on him! Fortunately, nothing improper happened, and he moved out after a few months.

There were three gas stations in the area, a barbershop (Birdwell's), and a small grocery store (Jack's Market). The owner of Jack's Market was George Pashal. What I remember about George is he had a head full of black hair! Best of all, he was really good to us kids. He would let us fill up the Coke coolers and then give us two or three dollars. There was a Dairy Dip in the neighborhood as well, and Mama often asked me to go there and get her favorite treat: a banana milk shake.

McCabe Park was near our house, and the local kids played there and in the creek that ran through the golf course. Best of all was the tunnel, which had been built under Forty-Sixth Street and Murphy Road back in the thirties. It was wide enough to drive a car through. We boys played there often, but luckily I never saw a car down there. The tunnel was about a fourth of a mile long and very dark. One game we played at night was to see who was brave enough to make it alone all the way through, armed with only one lighted candle.

So there were lots of fun things for a little boy to do, even without much money. It was kind of like living in the made-for-TV town of Mayberry, up to and including some of its similar town characters.

Michael A Davis

The thing I remember most about living in the Nebraska house was the loneliness. There seemed to be no father and no mother, because she was always working second-shift jobs. Mostly I remember being home by myself.

I did join Cub Scouts, and I used to imagine Papa would surprise me one day by coming to one of my meetings. But he never did. He did leave a lot of neat tools behind when he left us for good in 1960, however, and I would often play with them—a rake, a hard hat, wheelbarrow, a flashlight. I remember thinking, *What would a man do with all this stuff?* Now I know they were some of the tools he used in his carpentry and building trade.

My mother lived out her days there in the Nebraska house, thirty-one years altogether. Through the years, William was the one who kept the closest relationship with Mama. She especially loved the Grand Ole Opry, and he took her there often. Her favorite country stars were Charlie Rich and Bill Anderson. She was a small-statured lady, never weighing more than 125 pounds, but she loved eating out. Her favorite restaurant was Sylvan Park Restaurant. Mama died on April 29, 1997. She was seventy-nine years old.

As for Papa? We never heard from him again. And him telling Mama he had been in the Army for twenty years before he met her? Well we now know that was just another example of a ramblin' man trying to explain his ramblin'.

* * *

The only thing our father left us was alone.

In 1960, when he did finally leave us for good (pun intended), he headed north and west to St. Louis. This was also the year his mother died. Family members have since told me she was a hard woman. Maybe that's why he turned out like he did.

Not having a father helped make me strong in several ways. I learned to be self-reliant and determined to persevere when things got tough. Being able to find blessings in not having a father is a good thing. And I have God to thank for that, because His word taught me,

"And we know that all things work together for good to them that love God, to them who are the called according to his purpose."

— Romans 8:28 (American King James)

Bits and Pieces

Wilma Parsons was born July 2, 1918, in the hills of Tennessee, near Crossville. With four older brothers and one sister, she was the youngest of the six. Customary of the times, the spot was called Parsons Ridge, named after the family living there. This was a poor family that lived on the land as best they could.

Her dad, Mark Parsons, was born August 10, 1878, in Cumberland, Tennessee, and died there on November 29, 1959. He married Eva J. Cole, who was born in Crossville, Tennessee, in 1903. In addition to my mother, Wilma, the other children were Fred, Carson, Homer, Hubert, and Ruby.

When she was twenty-three, Wilma had an affair with a married man, last name Crabtree, and got pregnant with her first child, Clifford, who was born March 5, 1942.

Three years later, she got pregnant from a relationship with Max Flores. They got married on July 11, 1944, at the insistence of *his* parents. He was thirty-three. My half-brother, Stanley Franklin Flores, was born February 27, 1945. This marriage was annulled, or they divorced, soon after his birth.

And then along came Jones.

I mean Papa.

Childhood Memories

It was my job to gather the eggs from the chicken coop. I guess everyone knows if you raise chickens, you have one, and only one, rooster. Ours was a Rhode Island Red. He was big. And he was mean. (Is there any other kind?)

So this particular day, I was about eight or nine at the time, I went out back to the chicken coop, and the rooster started after me. I screamed and yelled for William to help. When the rooster saw William, he took out after him instead, so William jumped up on top of a picnic table to get away from him. Papa had built it a few years before leaving us.

I ran off to the house. I was supposed to get help for William. But I couldn't find Mama. And then I forgot.

William stayed up on that table for about forty-five minutes. When he finally jumped down, that patient and mean old rooster jumped on him again, flogged his wings all around his head, clawed his back, and pecked his neck all the way to the house.

Mama yelled at both of us when she found out, because all the eggs got smashed and scattered all around the yard. William didn't speak to me the rest of the day.

— Diane Davis Mittler, October 2011

*   *   *

Well I will never forget the day we were all sitting at the breakfast table when suddenly, we heard very loud, very strange noises at the back door. To us kids it sounded like the boogeyman was pounding on the door, coming to get us for sure! The next thing we knew, we see two long mule legs pushing open the screen door! It was our little burro, Peepot*, that Papa had brought home to Clifford as a present after one of his "absences."

Of course Papa was now long gone, and we barely had enough money to buy food ourselves, and our poor little burro was hungry, because we had no money to buy his food. I guess he smelled the food and thought he'd just get some for himself. We loved that little donkey so much! I don't remember what, but we rummaged around the kitchen and fridge and managed to find something for him to eat.

We had to keep a pretty close watch on him to make sure no one came along and took him to sell to the glue factory, which was about five blocks away. Every afternoon around 3 p.m., they started up their "equipment," and we could smell this awful horse/animal/death smell. It is s something I will never forget.

I never want to smell that smell again.

— William Davis, October 2011

*We named him that because . . . well, I think you can imagine why.

*   *   *

And then there was the time I tried to teach William how to ride his two-wheel bike. He was about seven; I was fourteen. I guess I should have known better. Maybe you can picture this little kid, wobbling down this really steep hill, trying to maintain control and balance his bike. He didn't, of course. Keep his balance, that is. And got his foot caught in the front wheel spokes to boot. *That's* when he crashed into a big bush that happened to get in his way. And *that's* when the hornet's nest fell. Mama heard him screaming and came running. And *that's* when the hornets took after William and Mama.

And when Papa got home that night and looked at the flat front tire on the bike, *that's* when he got mad and whupped us both!

— Stanley Davis, October 2011

*   *   *

A Witch Named Snuffy Gun

Yep. Uh-huh. Snuffy Gun. That was her name, all right. I saw her. Yep. Mama told us not to go in that ol' house. But we did anyway.

It was the fall of 1963, and there was hardly anyone left in the neighborhood, so most of the houses were vacant. And that witch, Ol' Snuffy Gun, was livin' there, just like Mama said. That witch was waitin' for us the night me and Diane and William sneaked into that ol' house. Of course our two dogs, Ding Pot and Renny, followed us.

Most folks in the neighborhood had already moved away. Interstate 40 was being built, and it was coming right down our street. Some men kept coming to the house, telling Mama we had to move. But she just ignored them. I think she was waitin' for Papa to come back and help us find another place to live. 'Cept he never did.

I remember it was really dark that night. And creepy, as we snuck up to that ol' house. We opened the door, real slow like, and crept inside. And then, suddenly, there she was!

Ol' Snuffy Gun! Just like Mama said. She raised up off the floor where she was hidin' an' we saw her.

The next thing I knew, me and Diane and William were runnin' over each other, tryin' to get out of there. They were bigger 'n faster than me and knocked me down, and I tore my pants on a nail. I was so scared! I jumped up and then fell over Ding Pot. I heard him growling as I ran out the door. I knew he was protectin' me the best he could. An' then he hightailed it out the door, too. We ran outta there like it was a jailhouse break!

I never knew kids and dogs could run so fast! Somehow we got away before she got us. I don't know how Mama knew Ol' Snuffy Gun lived there, but I sure ain't never goin' back to ask.

— Michael Davis, age eight

*   *   *

This little story of Ol' Snuffy Gun has become a family story passed down to William's, Diane's, and my children and their children.

The one thing we kids didn't realize back then, and Mama neglected to explain, was that because we lived only three blocks from the train tracks, hobos would frequently come into the almost vacant neighborhood and camp out for a few days or weeks. Several years passed before it dawned on us kids that Ol' Snuffy Gun and some old hobo were one and the same and that we probably scared him just as much as he scared us.

Wilma Parson Davis 1944

Wilma Parson Davis and Max Flores 1944

Clifford and Stanislavsky
512 Thomas St. Harrisburg Tennessee

Clifford and Stanley Davis
512 Thomas St. Harrisburg Tennessee

Michael A Davis

Wilma Davis and son Stanley Davis
512 Thomas St. Luxemburg Tennessee 1947

Me and my dog Delaware ave Nashville Tennessee 1963

Michael A Davis

I Remember Mama

Mama was a simple country girl with simple country interests. Well kind of. For one thing, she *loved* professional wrestling. She would take us almost every Tuesday night to the Hippodrome on West End. The Hippodrome is long gone; now the spot is occupied by the Holiday Inn.

Back then, in 1966–67, however, it was great fun for me to get to go. We got to see wrestlers like Bear-Cat Brown, Lynn Rossi, the Mighty Yankees, the Scuffling Hillbillies (Rip Collins and Chuck Conley), and everybody's favorite, Jackie Fargo. They would pass out autographed pictures of all the wrestlers. Let me tell you, that was a big deal to a nine-year-old kid!*

The thing I didn't realize back then was the renters took us. Which is to say, I believe they paid for our tickets. A "perk," you might say, of having mostly male renters. One in particular I remember: Charlie Moore. He was pretty nice to us kids.

One of the best wrestling events we ever attended was the night Jerry Lee Lewis came and performed after all the wrestling was over. What a showman he was! He stood there at that piano and jumped around and played all over that keyboard. He sure seemed like he was having a lot of fun! And we sure had fun watching him!

Back then, the Hippodrome was also used as a skating rink in the winter months. It only cost fifty cents, and we would go on Friday nights. Mama never learned to drive, so we would pester Charlie 'til he agreed to take us.

— Michael Davis, October 2011

*The fifty-three-year-old "kid" still has all the wrestling pictures. So that was life then.

4

This Is Now

| 4509 Wyoming Today | 4709 Nebraska Today |

These houses were built on opposite sides of Charlotte Avenue, Charlotte being what I call the DMZ Zone. On the prison side of Charlotte is the Nations neighborhood, where the Wyoming house is located, and where I regularly got beat up on my way home from school. Getting to and from school required me to traverse other streets—other "nations"—and that meant a fight.

The other side of Charlotte, known as Sylvan Park, remains a desirable neighborhood of old, well-kept Victorian homes, and this is where we lived in the Nebraska house. I could ride my bike through the tunnel right by my house and come out on Murphy Road, which was, and still is, filled with small shops, a Diary Queen, and a "meat and three" restaurant—Sylvan Park Restaurant—which still serves the best country cookin' in Nashville.

But what about the kids from this second family—the Tennessee Troupe? Where are they now? What are they willing to share?

Bits and Pieces of the Lives of the Children of Wilma Parsons and the Ramblin' Man Named Robert Benjamin Davis

My oldest brother, *Clifford McArthur Davis,* is sixty-nine years old and still in good health. He lives in Hendersonville, Tennessee. He's married and has one son and one daughter.

My brother *Stanley Franklin Davis* is sixty-five years old. He lives in Murfreesboro, Tennessee. He worked at Avco Aircraft Corporation for forty-two years but is now retired. He loves to cook and has two children, a son and daughter.

Next is *William Roy Davis*. He was born in 1952. Sadly, his wife, Deborah, passed in 2011. They were married in 1971 and have two sons, William Ted and Matthew Brad Davis. William's hobbies are reading and collecting old pictures.

My sister, *Wanda Diane Davis,* was born in 1954 in Nashville, Tennessee. She has a nursing degree and works as surgical nurse at Williamson County Medical Center in Franklin, Tennessee. She is married to Dale Mittler. She has two daughters, Tonya and Keeley, and a son, Jason Todd. Diane is a fun-loving, happy person, loves riding her bicycle, and has a great love of animals.

And then there's me—*Michael Anthony Davis*. I was born in 1959. I have two daughters, Krista and Kayla, and a son, Michael. My wife, Teresa, and I live in Murfreesboro, Tennessee. I love Vanderbilt football. I teach blended family classes at the World Outreach Church in Murfreesboro (imagine that!).

I am indebted to my family for their love and to God for His many blessings.

Cohn high school 2011

Me and my friends at Cohn high school 1976

Me with Ronnie and uncle Hurbert Parson 1976

Papa was a Rolling Stone

Forty-Sixth
Street and Murphy Road

To a little boy growing up there in the seventies, this was like the Mayberry of the South. Shops, shoe repair, restaurant, and the Dairy Dip were all within walking or riding distance from home. Forty-Sixth Street dead ends into McCabe Park to the right of this picture. (Arrow points to Jack's Market.)

Jacks market 2011

Mccabe park and golf course entrance 2011

Mccabe park and golf course entrance2011

Michael A Davis

Riding my bike home from the store or playing in the park and seeing this structure lit up at night was a scary thing indeed.

The Tennessee State Prison is a former correctional facility located near downtown Nashville, Tennessee. Opened in 1898, the prison has been closed since 1992. It has been the location for the films *Nashville, Marie, Ernest Goes to Jail, Against the Wall, The Green Mile, The Last Castle,* and Pillar's *Bring Me Down* video. Most recently, VH1's Celebrity Paranormal Project filmed there for the third episode of the series (titled "The Warden") as well as the last episode of the first season (titled "Dead Man Walking"). The prison was referred to as "The Walls Maximum Security Prison" in both episodes to protect the location's privacy.

The proposed prison design called for the construction of a fortress-like structure patterned after the penitentiary at Auburn, New York, made famous for the lockstep marching, striped prisoner uniforms, nighttime solitary confinement, and daytime congregate work under strictly enforced silence. The new Tennessee prison contained 800 small cells, each designed to house a single inmate. In addition, an administration building and other smaller buildings for offices, warehouses, and factories were built within the twenty-foot (6.15m) high, three-foot (1 m) thick rock walls. The plan also provided for a working farm outside the walls and mandated a separate system for younger offenders to isolate them from older, hardened criminals.

The prison was built by Enoch Guy Elliott, who was married to Lady Ida Beasley Elliott (Missionary to Burma). Gov. Turney made Enoch Guy Elliott the Chief Warden of the old prison and then, during the building of the second prison, Enoch used primarily prison labor to build the new prison.

Construction costs for this second Tennessee State Penitentiary exceeded $500,000 ($12.3 million in 2007 dollars), not including the price of the land. The prison's 800 cells opened to receive prisoners on February 12, 1898, and that day admitted 1,403 prisoners, creating immediate overcrowding. To a greater or lesser extent, overcrowding persisted throughout the next century. The original Tennessee State Penitentiary on Church Street was demolished later that year, and salvageable materials were used in the construction of outbuildings at the new facility, creating a physical link from 1830 to the present.

Every convict was expected to defray a portion of the cost of incarceration by performing physical labor. Within two years, inmates worked up to sixteen hours per day for meager rations and unheated, unventilated sleeping quarters. The State also contracted with private companies to operate factories inside the prison walls using convict labor.

The Tennessee State Penitentiary had its share of problems. In 1902, seventeen prisoners blew out the end of one wing of the prison, killing one inmate and allowing the escape of two others who were never recaptured. Later, a group of inmates seized control of the segregated white wing and held it for eighteen hours before surrendering. In 1907 several convicts commandeered a switch engine and drove it through a prison gate. In 1938 inmates staged a mass escape. Several serious fires ignited at the penitentiary, including one that destroyed the main dining room. Riots occurred in 1975 and 1985.

In 1989 the Tennessee Department of Correction opened a new penitentiary, the River Bend Maximum Security Institution at Nashville. The old Tennessee State Penitentiary closed in June 1992. As part of the settlement in a class action suit, Grubbs v. Bradley (1983), the Federal Court issued a permanent injunction prohibiting the Tennessee Department of Correction from ever again housing inmates at the Tennessee State Prison.

This is me and my brothers and sister standing where our Delaware house used to be. I-40 above went right through the middle of our property:

Me, Diane, William, and Clifford
December 2011

These are the railroad tracks at the end of our street, Delaware. Hobos hung out and rode the rails or camped out in vacant houses when people moved out because of the pending I-40 road construction.

This is the signage above the section of I-40 that replaced our Delaware house.

Michael A Davis

Mama's Favorite Restaurant—

Sylvan Park Restaurant, 4502 Murphy Road,
Nashville, TN, 615-292-9275

(The Best Country Cookin' in Town—Then and Now)

People Eating in Restaurant

Sample Plate Lunch

Mama and her friend, Jim Oates, 1986 (and this Old Victorian is still one of the prettiest homes in the Sylvan Park neighborhood)

And Whatever Happened to Jackie Fargo? Well, he was alive and well in 2009 . . .

The wrestler: Jackie Fargo will be inducted this weekend into NWA hall of fame
By Susan Shinn, Published Sunday, August 02, 2009 2:00 AM
sshinn@salisburypost.com

CHINA GROVE—Jackie Fargo steps off the porch on a tree-lined China Grove street to greet visitors. His long, silver hair carefully combed back, he's wearing a shiny red shirt, jeans that seem a little big for him and black, thick-soled shoes favored by men his age. And he's also wearing a sequined belt buckle, made for him years ago. A couple of the spangles have fallen off. Professional wrestlers never retire, it seems. The glory days are always just beneath the surface.

Fargo, 79, along with his brother, the late Jack Faggart, who wrestled as Sonny Fargo, and Don Kalt, who wrestled as Don Fargo, will be inducted Friday, Aug. 7, into the National Wrestling Alliance's hall of fame. It's part of the NWA Wrestling Legends FanFest weekend.

Other members of the 2009 Hall of Heroes class include Playboy Gary Hart, Chief Wahoo McDaniel, Blackjack Mulligan, Nelson Royal and Lance Russell.

Ceremonies will be held at the Hilton University Place in Charlotte. The third-annual event is already sold out.

"People want to know the inside stuff," says Howard Platt, a local radio personality and wrestling fan. "People are fascinated with that. It's a nostalgia thing."

Stepping into his house, Fargo leads visitors into a darkened hall, lit by a single naked bulb. There's a poster-sized picture of him shaking hands with Muhammed Ali. There are certificates of all types, but the one he's proudest of is dated July 25, 1966.

Way before the days of Make-a-Wish, Fargo met a young boy sick with cancer, whose life's dream was to meet the wrestler Jackie Fargo.

"I have never seen such a smile on a young man," Jackie says, his memory undimmed.

Doctors said the boy had only a couple of months to live, but after meeting Fargo, he lived a year.

"That just broke my heart," he says. "He was such a lovely little fellow."

It's fair to say that Fargo has mellowed over the years.

He started his professional wrestling career in 1949—60 years ago.

He had wrestled at the Cannon YMCA before that, and went to Goldsboro for the state championship.

A promoter asked him, "Ever thought about being a professional wrestler?"

"Gee whiz," Fargo says. "I was making $7 a week. I dressed in the back of my car."

Fargo spent his most of his life in Tennessee. He wrestled all over the world—Japan, Korea, Honolulu, included.

But he was always proud to be from China Grove, and retired here in 1986.

His older brother Jack joined him in the profession. Their given name was Faggart, but promoters told them it wasn't a wrestling name. Fargo was known as "Honey Boy Fargo" for his blond locks and later the Fabulous Jackie Fargo when he cut a few 45 records with friends in Nashville.

Jack became Sonny Fargo. He wrestled and later refereed matches.

He and Sonny were the first professional wrestlers to sell out Madison Square Garden in the 1960s. In later years, Fargo legally changed his name to his wrestling moniker. He asked his daddy if it was all right before doing so. In his profession, he was a "good guy" and a "bad guy."

"I was tough," Fargo says. "I could back up what I said."

In the '50s, he had the chance to wrestle in Havana, making $250 a week—all expenses paid.

"It was so nice over there," he says. "It was just absolutely fabulous. The Cubans liked wrestling and gambling and sports. You can't name a place I haven't been. But give me good ol' China Grove!"

In the '60s, Elvis Presley came to see Fargo wrestle in Las Vegas. One of Fargo's three daughters has that picture somewhere. He recently returned from an appearance in Tullahoma, Tenn. So he can't really stay retired.

"They won't let me," Fargo says.

He'll go as long as they call—and offer money.

Before long, Fargo's nephew, Obie Faggart, stops by with details of the upcoming FanFest appearance. Faggart grew up in the wrestling world, driving his daddy to matches, doing his homework when he got there.

"I got to do things other kids didn't get to do," Faggart says. He and his sister, Debbie Parson, will accept Jack Faggart's award.

"It will be an honor," he says.

Jack Faggart died Aug. 21, 2008. Fargo misses his brother but is close to his nephew.

"I love you, bud," he says, as Faggart leaves.

Fargo is down almost 100 pounds from his wrestling weight of 270.

"You had to eat the right things," he says. "I used to run 10 to 12 miles a day, 6 days a week."

He ate potatoes and bananas to keep his weight up, and lifted weights.

"I used to be a mean guy," he says, showing off pictures of him and his long, blond hair. He didn't like to be teased about it.

"I expected it," he says, "but don't make a fool out of me in front of somebody."

Fargo's signature move was called "The Atomic Drop."

He demonstrates it on Jon Lakey, Post photographer. (Lakey is a bit tentative, but goes along with it.)

You come up from behind your opponent on the left side, so they can't hit you with their left hand. You lift them up and drop them onto your knee. The impact on the spine momentarily stuns them—long enough for you to pin them and win the match. Fargo acknowledges he was hurt over the years. All former professional wrestlers have bad knees, he says.

He's got a knot in his right shoulder—it was broken four times.

"That's part of the game," he says.

Although Fargo still loves wrestling he says, "I'm ashamed of it today. I watch it for one reason, and that is to criticize."

And when he watches a tag team in action, he's thinking the same thing every time. "I could beat both of them in 30 seconds."

"They don't have what it takes today," Fargo says. "Back in my day, they wouldn't have been around one match."

He throws up his hand as a public works truck rumbles by.

"Hey fellas!" he says.

Fargo's the type who never meets a stranger.

"No siree," he says. "I'm very proud of that, too."

He and Judy, his wife of 34 years, live in a small house that belonged to his family. He says he wouldn't take a million dollars for Sassy, their 5-year-old Yorkie. She grunts like a pig when she gets excited. Fargo golfs and travels and visits casinos.

"I'm not going to sit around and let myself go," he says.

Is he still fabulous?

He holds Sassy close.

"More than ever!" Fargo says with a smile.

5

And Then There Were Five . . . More

So where was Papa from the time he left my mother, Wilma, in 1959 until he met and married Mardella Sue Roberts in 1963? I can't say for sure, but I do have a theory.

Papa had cousins in Kansas City, Missouri, which is one hundred fifty miles from St. Louis. Moberly is about halfway between. I can imagine him stopping at a local bar (beer garden) in Moberly, a likely spot to meet the locals, having a few friendly beers, and asking them if they knew of any construction jobs in the area. He ran into Mardella's father there, one of the locals and regular customers at the bar, who was also engaged in the construction industry, and he was looking to marry off his daughter.

Now that I have met these relatives myself, I know Papa was visiting back and forth between Kansas City and St. Louis during 1961 and 1962. So that is a possible explanation.

Regardless, one way or another, he does meet Mardella. She was twenty; he was sixty-four. He told her he had been in the navy for twenty years. That was as good an explanation as any, I guess.

As for Mardella, she was young, naive, and trusting. Besides, from everything I've learned about my papa, he could always turn on the charm when it suited his purposes. So I'm guessing she wasn't too concerned about the age difference between herself and Papa.

So Papa and Mardella married in 1963. They moved to St. Charles, Missouri, at this time and lived in a trailer park outside St. Louis. They had five children: Wanda Diane, Michael Lonnie, Marcella A. (Marci), Brian Edward, and Steven C. For a time, Mardella's younger sister lived with them. After Papa died in 1970, Mardella and the children moved back to Moberly. She has lived there ever since.

When I visited Mardella in 2008, she told me Papa named all their children. It's hard to believe he would name some of these children the same names as his other children.* I guess along with his bad temper, he had a bad memory, too. Mardella never remarried. She is sixty-five years old.

She has not revealed much about those years with Papa except to say he was a hardworking man. She told me he worked as a bricklayer on the St. Louis Arch during the period 1965–1969. It must have been hard at his age, and he died a year later. This is something hard for me to think about.

When I talked with Mardella's daughter, my half-sister Marci (Marcella), she told me Papa got so mad at the teacher one day when they lived in St. Louis he went to the school and took her sister right out of the classroom.

That's the kind of thing he did that always got him in trouble. And it was why they moved from St. Louis to Moberly, Missouri, about a hundred miles from Kansas City. He had relatives there in Kansas City; I guess he wanted to be closer to them.

Finding Mardella and her children has been one of the unexpected blessings resulting from my desire to find my father and tell his story. Some things never change, though, and I learned these children suffered the consequences of Papa's volatile temper just like the rest of us did. Of course, he still had the habit of coming and going as he pleased from time to time.

But getting to know Mardella has been a joy. She is the dearest, sweetest person and has kept in touch with me from the time we first met. She has loved me like a son and sends me cards and letters all the time. Since Papa's death, she has lived on his Social Security benefits. Mostly she only talks about the "good" things she remembers. I guess that's a good thing.

*Ironically enough, when I started searching online records, I found these names that were the same or similar to the brothers and sister I knew. So Papa's quirky method for naming his children helped me find the rest of my family.

Update: November 2011

My wife and sister, Diane, and I spent this past Thanksgiving holiday with Mardella in Moberly. She remains in good health and is an amazingly kind, warmhearted person. She loves church, writing letters, and life itself.

*   *   *

Michael A Davis

Moberly water tank 2011

Moberly city street 2011

Michael A Davis

Trailer park where papa and Marcella lived in 1963

Creek beside Marcella house in trailer park

Marcella and kids live after papa died in 1970

Marcella Davis and dog

Michael A Davis

Bits and Pieces of the Five More

Wanda Diane Davis was born in Moberly, Missouri, in 1964. She went to college, got married, and has two daughters and one son. She lives in Texas, has started several businesses, and is having fun doing it.

Michael Lonnie Davis was born in 1965 and died in 2010.

Marcella A. Davis was born in 1966 and lives in Cairo, Missouri, just outside Moberly. She works for the phone company. She is a strong-willed person with a positive attitude about life. She is married and has one son and one daughter. She loves outdoor activities and treasures her family.

Brian Edward Davis was born in 1968.

Steven C. Davis was born in 1969.

6

Epilogue

The sounds of the cemetery workmen digging a new grave a few feet away jolt me from my reverie back to the present, and once more my eyes focus on the gravestone before me.

As I rise from my cramped kneeling position, my knees rebel in pain from bending so long, and I realize I have been lost in my thoughts for some time. Straightening my knees, I am enveloped by a new feeling that overtakes me as I look once more at the final resting spot of my father.

"I do forgive you," I say in wonderment as I recognize this new emotion squeezing through my heart. Then, as though a great weight has been lifted, an overwhelming sense of relief floods my senses.

My church had always taught me forgiveness benefits the forgiver as much or more than the one you forgive. 'Til now, I had never experienced it in such a personal way.

I check the time—1:33 p.m. Time to leave.

Heading for the parking lot, emotionally drained, I find my car and drive off to the airport to catch my plane back to Murfreesboro, Tennessee. Quickly parking my rental car at Budget's Quick Drop, I rush to my boarding gate, hoping the traffic jam I had encountered along the way has not caused me to be late for boarding. Glancing at my watch, I am startled to see it has stopped exactly at 1:33 p.m.

* * *

Here in Ravenel, South Carolina, in White Church Cemetery, we discover the end of the complicated and extraordinary life of Robert Benjamin Davis, born in Charleston in 1899, died in St. Charles, Missouri, in 1970, and buried in Ravenel, South Carolina.

—Robert Benjamin Davis of Charleston, South Carolina, who married Virginia Carrow of Adams Run, South Carolina, in 1921, moved her to Daytona Beach, Florida, where he fathered twelve children and then simply walked away one day in May of 1945.

—Robert Benjamin Davis, who in September of that same year, married Wilma Parsons in Nashville, Tennessee, fathered five more children, and then in 1960, once more simply walked away when Michael, the youngest son of this marriage, was three months old.

—Robert Benjamin Davis, who in 1963, when he was sixty-four years old, married twenty-year-old Mardella Sue Roberts in St. Charles, Missouri, and managed to father five more children before he died in 1970.

The end of a life. But not the end of the story.

For Michael, the youngest son of the second family, in some ways it has been the beginning. The beginning of a life free from anger and pain and confusion. Getting here has taken years of research and discovery. Still there are some unanswered questions. For instance, just where was his dad from 1961 to 1963?

But through these years of searching, Michael has discovered family. Locating twenty-two—and counting—half-brothers and half-sisters he never knew has been a joy and blessing worth the painful journey, he says.

His father was a complex man, full of contradictions: hardworking bricklayer, musician, outdoorsman, and . . . wanderer and philanderer. Full of laughter at times, viciously mean at others.

Retracing the footsteps of his father, discovering and recording the events in the extraordinary life of this man, has been a painful but healing experience. Learning who his earthly father was—the good, the bad, the ugly—has filled the empty place in his heart where dad memories are supposed to be. Michael gives the credit for "bringing him through" these painful revelations to a place of forgiveness and freedom to his heavenly Father . . . God.

In sharing his journey, his story, Michael hopes you will find encouragement, forgiveness, and inspiration for your own life journey.

7

Amelia's Diary

In the Beginning . . .

I was asked to start my family's life story from when I knew it began.

In 1845 there was a famine in Ireland—it was called the potato famine (Irish potato), and people were starving to death. So they started leaving their homeland for the New World.

My mother's grandmother, Elizabeth Frances Miller, and her husband, Abraham Howard, were two of the Irish people wanting to get away from the famine.

They got on a ship, and when they got to New York City, the officials wouldn't let them disembark, because there was already too many Irish people there. So they turned them away. The ship sailed down the coast to Charleston, South Carolina. The officials were turning people back there, too. But the ship's captain said they needed food and water before they could go further.

While these supplies were being put on the ship, my great-grandfather took his pregnant wife and threw her overboard and dove in after her. But the officials had seen him, so they sent men to bring them back. Now my great-grandmother's baby was not due yet, but the strain of the voyage and the shock of being thrown overboard caused her to go into labor. So by the time the officials found them on the boat, they had a child—an American child—and the baby couldn't be sent back to be brought up in Ireland. So my great-grandparents got to stay in South Carolina.

Not much is known about my father's origins except his people were sent to the New World as bonded people. His grandfather was taken out of debtor's prison (in those days it was a prison offence to owe a debt and not pay), sent to America to work off seven years of debt, and was bonded to a brick—and stonemason.

So now both families are in America; my father's people in Charleston, South Carolina, and my mother's people in St. John's Island, South Carolina. Great-Grandpa Howard was a wheelwright. He made wheels for wagons and later built buggies.

All this took place twenty years before the Civil War.

As luck would have it, if they had not been turned back at the New York Port of Entry, today we would be Yankees.

Great-Grandma Elizabeth was twenty-nine at the time she landed in America and was forty-five years old when the Civil War broke out, living in the first state to leave the Union, South Carolina. Her husband and her neighbors were in the war at its beginning.

The war lasted four years; four long hard years for the women left behind. My great-grandmother had eight children by the time the war started.

But now the South had changed a great deal. Southerners were not allowed to own anything. If you did manage to catch a wild pig and raise him before time to butcher him, the Yankee soldiers would come and confiscate him or anything else you valued.

The Yankees recruited lots of blacks, because at that time, if you were rich, you didn't have to go in the army, you could pay someone else to go in your place, and that's what a lot of Yankees did—they hired black men to take their place.

But four years later, the war is over, and the men are coming home. In order to come home, they had to turn in their guns—their swords and knives were broken—so many men had part of their swords, and one of them found a blunderbuss. It was a short shotgun with a large mouth, about three to four inches across. It had been broken but on the way home, but he managed to fix it.

Back at home, the Yankee Army, mostly blacks and led by a black sergeant, came to my great-grandfather's home. Knowing the war was over and that the men would soon be home, he raped my great-grandmother and—the ultimate disgrace—tied her nude to a tree in the yard in the pouring rain! The soldiers told the children if they untied her, they would stop on their way back and kill them all.

The next morning before daylight, her husband, Great-Grandpa Howard, came home, along with all the men still living from their regiment. My great-grandmother was in so much disgrace she could not live with the shame. The other men went and got their wives to console her, but they could not. Early the next day, while everyone thought she was sleeping, she got the only gun in the neighborhood, put the muzzle in her mouth, and shot her head off!

Michael A Davis

Later that day, two of the children who had stood by their mother the whole day she was tied to the tree caught pneumonia and died soon after.

My great-grandfather Howard was raving and ranting like a devil in torment for days. And then one day, his neighbors found him squatting on the ground with his broken sword in one hand and a whet stone in the other.

From then on, people would see him everywhere, always doing the same thing—squatting, sharpening the sword. The black Yankee troopers saw him—they called him crazy and ignored him. But he had method to his madness. Eventually everyone forgot about him and began taking up their own lives again.

The Yankee sergeant who had brought his men to my great-grandfather's house was sure surprised when Great-Grandpa jumped up in front of him one day as he was crossing a field of tall grass. Great-Grandpa Abraham shoved the broken sword (which was now sharpened on both sides) into the sergeant's belly and ran around him. He said later, when he was walking away, the guy just stood staring at him in amazement. Until he fell dead.

No one saw what happened, and my great-grandfather took his family and moved out on one of the islands near St. John's Island. He remarried and took up living again.

My grandmother, Elizabeth Frances, had nineteen brothers and sisters, two fathers, and three mothers in her lifetime.

Old War Stories

Back then, every family had one. Here's ours.

Our grandmother's father, Abraham Howard, said he didn't know for sure, but he really believed he had only shot one Yankee during the "great war." The reason, he said, was because most of the time you were shooting across fields, and you couldn't really be sure if you hit anyone.

But one day he was in an awful battle—Chickamauga—and he jumped into one end of a ditch. At the same time, a Yankee soldier jumped in at the other end. They both fired at the same time. The Yankee missed, and Great-Grandpa Howard jumped right back out after he fired, so if he killed anyone in the war, that would have been the only one he knew of.

But then he said he killed a lot of them *after* the war. Then he got home and found out they had turned that crazy General Sherman loose, and he burned everything he couldn't tote off.

So it left a lot of bad feeling in the South after the war.

Great-Grandpa Howard had a daughter—my great-aunt Carrie—and she was an awfully big woman. She took care of most of the family while the men were away. She had heard that the Union soldiers were "having their way" with the women, so she got prepared.

Sure enough, one day three black soldiers came by. Carrie was quite nice to them. When they wanted more than she was offering, she asked if they would come into her house, one at a time. She had a Dutch door; you could open both pieces or top or bottom half. She told them she had nailed the top shut. So they had to get on their hands and knees to come in.

As they came in, she hit them on the head with an iron skillet. And killed them.

One . . . by . . . one.

Then she had her field prepared, and planted them under her new pear slips. The pear slips did great! The next year, people who tasted the pears said they were the sweetest pears they had ever tasted. Carrie would always smile and say she had our new government to thank for the nice pears.

Michael A Davis

For my grandmother, Elizabeth, the hurt from the Civil War never ended. She would cry when she told us about it—just like it had just happened.

The first time Yankee soldiers came to Charleston, the boys training to be in the service at the Citadel and their teachers beat the Yankees. But the Citadel boys let them ride their horses and keep their side arms and got a "gentleman's agreement" that they (the Yankees) would not come back to Charleston.

Well I guess you know you can't trust a Yankee, so when the Yankees got out of Charleston, they met up with General Sherman. So these Yankee troops not only came back, they made the Citadel men there walk down the streets with their brass buttons torn from their uniforms. Then they went on with Sherman and burnt Charleston, just like they did in Atlanta. And now history says Sherman burnt the South from Atlanta to the sea.

And he did.

Only he had to fight old men and women and children to do it, so it shouldn't have been too much of a job.

But all that's over now, and we have to live together. But we do know the North lost 400,000 men. We lost 200,000. And the South won every major battle for three and a half of the four years the war was on.

Friends of the Family

(My mother told me this story when I was about thirty-five years old.)

You probably know the Seminole Indians that we have in Florida was the only Indian tribe that didn't surrender to the United States. That's why the government can't tell them what to do.

My father met their Indian chief—I remember he called him John—when he went to college in Charleston, South Carolina.

So when they finished college, Chief John invited Daddy to come and visit the tribe encampment down in the Everglades. This would have been in the 1920s. So my mother and father went down there and stayed with them for a while.

The Chief sent some of his men to show them the way in. That's because there were no roads anywhere else in Florida. The Indian roads were underwater at this time, and the Indians were the only ones who knew where the roads were.

My mother—who stayed pregnant almost every year from then on and finally had twelve children—was pregnant with her first baby. Back then no one ever went to a doctor to have a baby. You just got help from another woman, usually a neighbor.

So when the time came for my mother to have her baby, the women in the tribe took her out into the woods. They put a piece of material between two trees and fit the material under her belly so if she went to sleep she would still be held up. And they put food and water nearby. Sometimes it took a couple of days to have a kid. But then they all left. Mama was really scared. There were a lot of wild animals around then.

But what she didn't know was the other women were there, just out of sight. It was their custom, so they wouldn't embarrass you if you screamed. Which you did, of course. And then, too, if you didn't have a lot of people around, they figured you wouldn't waste a lot of time having the baby.

As soon as she had the baby, the women came back and cleaned up her and the baby and took them back to their camp.

My mother and father liked it there in the Indian camp, but it was a hard way to live. So they left and went to Central Florida. But they stayed in touch with these Indians for a long time.

Our Depression Story

Before the Great Depression, my mother and father lived in Charleston, South Carolina. One day Mom was outside, tending her children, when a little old lady she knew came by. Most people thought the little old lady was crazy. She asked my mom if she had money in the bank.

Mom said, "A little."

The little old lady told her, "I read in the cards that the banks is gonna bust. If you have any money in the bank, go get it."

Mom said maybe tomorrow she would.

The little old woman told her, "Tomorrow will be too late."

Mama asked Daddy what he thought. He thought, like everyone else, that the little old woman was crazy. But Mama got to thinking about it, and she went and took half the money, $750.00, out of the bank. That same afternoon, they left for Florida. While they were on their way, someone told them, "The banks' busted, and you can't get no money out."

Now in those days, it took five months to get from Charleston, South Carolina, to Daytona Beach, Florida. You went somewhere, you got stuck, you stayed there 'til someone else came along, they helped you out, you helped them out, and then you drove on until you got stuck again. There were no paved roads. Just dirt. And if it wasn't muddy, it was sandy. So wherever you got stuck, that's where you stayed til someone else came along.

So Mama and Daddy were in Allendale, south of Daytona, when they heard about the Depression. Not having anything to go back to, they decided to stay there.

Now Mama told Daddy about getting half the money out of the bank before they left. So they bought a three-bedroom house and lot for $500 and lived there for the next ten years. At least Mama did. Daddy had to leave to find work or food.

This was a terrible time in our country's history. Not too many people actually had money, so they mostly traded for what they wanted and for what they needed. When I came along, I didn't think anything of it; mostly we traded all the time.

My grandmother came to live with us about this time. She stayed with us off and on for the remainder of her life.

Now during those hard Depression years, that's about when I started my life. The story goes like this.

My family's next-door neighbors lost all their money in the first part of 1929. The man just never could get over it, and in September in 1934, he committed suicide, leaving a pregnant wife and twelve-year old daughter. The man's wife ranted and raved all the time to my mother and grandmother about her terrible state and was always praying to God to kill her unborn child. She said if the child lived, she would kill it.

Now my mom was pregnant too. She was all gung-ho and happy about having a baby, and she had been traveling around a lot in an old truck with my father and leaving Grandma with the kids; there were nine at the time.

One day in May of 1935, my father, showing off for his friends, told my brother Neil to try to pick up the back end of a Model A Ford. My brother was twelve but big for his age and very strong. He always worked; he recycled metal. It wasn't long 'til his birthday, and he had asked my mom for a white metal milk truck he had seen in the hardware store. But it cost thirty-five cents; a lot of money then. But Neil still wanted it.

But on this particular day, my daddy was drinking, and someone said something about how big Neil was, and so Daddy made a bet with them that Neil could clear the ground picking up the truck.

Well Neil did it, just barely. But in doing so, he pulled his kidneys loose. Later that night, Neil died.

He bled to death.

On the day my parents buried Neil, they bought two cemetery lots with Neil's own money. Mom went to the hardware store and bought the white milk truck and wrapped it in white tissue paper and kept it with her for the next forty-five years, 'til her death. Sometimes she let us look at it, but nobody ever played with it.

While everyone was at Neil's funeral, one of the neighbors, a little bit of a woman, was keeping all the kids. They were all playing in the yard, putting pieces of wood and small rocks down on the ground where they jumped to see who could jump the furthest. Our neighbor's little girl found a stick and stuck it in the ground for her marker. But she stuck the flat side into the ground and left the sharp, pointed edge sticking up. When she jumped, she fell on it, and it stabbed her right in the heart. She pulled it out. It didn't bleed. Later, she wasn't feeling well. The little, old, neighbor woman had her lie down. When her mother came home from the funeral, she was dead. The little girl had died from internal bleeding.

Well her mother was really beside herself now. My parents gave her the other cemetery plot they had to buy when they bought Neil's, because the woman had nothing.

The next day Mama had her baby. It was dead. The kids came and got my grandma and told her the neighbor lady needed her; she was having her baby, too. Grandma took Mom's dead baby with her. When the neighbor lady's baby was born alive, my grandma gave her the dead baby and took the live one back to my mom.

The neighbor lady was so upset about the dead baby. Her prayers had been answered, but when she thought about it all—her husband dead and gone, her little girl dying, and now this—she walked with her baby to the river and just kept walking until she drowned. She is buried in Evergreen Cemetery, in Jacksonville, in the pauper's gravesite. So many people killed themselves in those days they often didn't even put names on the white crosses. So now the actual place is unknown.

My mother told me this story when I was forty-five years old, in 1980. Her mom told her when she was dying, in 1950, when Mama was forty-five. If Mama had waited another twelve hours to tell me this, it would have always been lost. Mama died before daylight the next day.

*   *   *

I never believed the person who gave you life was the only parent you could have. It's who stays up with you, cares about you, and gives you the foundation for your life. That's your mom and dad.

I do believe I got some things about myself from my real parents. I don't put too much on material things. If I have money, I spend it. If I don't have money, I don't spend. And I know I'm the only one who can make me happy. If I wait for someone else to make me happy, it may never happen.

Be happy!

The Great Hurricane of 1935

The great hurricane of 1935 hit on Labor Day.

In those days, the weather folks couldn't tell when a hurricane was going to hit until it was too late or just about at your feet. So my daddy had built a lean-to for us on the back of a block wall of a big factory in Miami. At this time, there were ten of us kids and one on the way. I was just four months old.

That morning the police drove their patrol cars through the town. The cars had speakers attached on the hoods, announcing that the storm that was coming. The police told everyone to go to the shelters set up by the city. Daddy's mom was staying with us at the time. She was an awful mean woman. She was like Daddy. Everyone who knew my daddy hated him, and you could tell what cloth he was cut from.

Papa headed for the lean-to, but Mama took her mother-in-law and us kids to the city shelter. Then Mama went back to the lean-to to get our daddy. He was too drunk to walk, so she stayed there in the lean-to with him through the hurricane. The eye of the storm came right over the city shelter. At one point, she ran back to the shelter to check on us kids and then went back to the lean-to with Daddy. At some point, the block wall of the factory fell the opposite way from the lean-to. What you'd call a right smart miracle, I'd say.

When it was over, the town was flattened as far as you could see. We could see big boats pushed miles up on land. Some years before, Mr. Flagler[2] had built this train track all the way from Jacksonville to Key West. The saddest thing of all was the fact that so many of the townspeople thought they had plenty of time to take one of the trains out of town, but when the last train left Key West, it only got to Lake Okeechobee.[3]

And then a wall of water hit the train and knocked it off the tracks. Hundreds of people drowned.

Now they have new bridges, but for a long time, the old rail bridges were the only way to get to Key West.

---

[2]   See "A Bit of History."
[3]   See "A Bit of History."

Michael A Davis

All About Me

I guess everybody pretty much thinks of their mothers as being different from "girls" they meet, but we're not. How do you think we know what y'all are doing? We probably did it ourselves or know someone who did.

So let me tell you about the real "me." I was pretty much an awful kid. I had a smart mouth. If anybody did anything to any of my brothers or sisters, I'd jump right in with my mouth and tell them what a lowlife they were. And then I'd usually have to outrun them. Or take a few licks.

I once told my dad to, "Pick on someone your own size," and he liked to have killed me. But he didn't stop me. If anything, he made me worse.

My father was an unusually cruel person—he blinded four of my brothers, one when he was eighteen. He blinded me in my right eye. But I asked for it. Like Mama always said, she never saw anybody want to get beat like I did. But I did distract my daddy.

I had a neighbor boy, Jimmy Arnold, who I taught a lot of stuff to. I got him to help me steal eggs from another neighbor. But what we didn't know was the hen was setting the eggs, and we cracked a hole in them and sucked them. I saw my daddy do that. Only these eggs had baby chicks about ready to hatch. And we got sick. I throwed up 'til I thought I'd die. Our grandma found us on the trail headed home, and she didn't whup us. She said we'd been punished enough.

Then my daddy made his daddy a big biddy pen. And Mr. Arnold put one hundred biddies in it. Well we stuck our hands in it, but the hens just ran over to the other side. So I talked Jimmy into squeezing into the top. We were small, and we got in there. We played with the biddies for hours. Then we saw it was getting late, so we tried to get out the way we got in. Only my daddy had put wire down into the cage, and it caught our clothes and we couldn't get out.

The whole top raised up, but we couldn't reach the latch. So we yelled and yelled, but no one heard us as the pen was way behind Jimmy's house.

Just before dark, my daddy came back there and found us. He raised the lid, took Jimmy out, put him on his hip, and beat his behind. Jimmy's father didn't believe in spanking kids, so this was Jimmy's first. His feet were just a-goin' when Daddy put him on the ground. He took off and didn't miss a step.

Daddy beat me when we got home.

Back then all the older kids skipped school in the summer. So one day I talked Jimmy into skipping. But in those days, they didn't tell you ahead of time when you were going to have a half-day. So we went swimming all day, and when we thought it was about time for school to be out, we walked home. And then we saw all the kids out playing in the road. So we hid behind our outhouse, because we knew we were going to get it. Everyone was looking for us. About dusk, my grandma came out to the outhouse, heard us crying, and made us come in the house. You know we got it then.

After we were grown, I went by to see Jimmy's mother. He's a preacher. She told me I taught him all the bad things he knew when he was a kid. Of course nobody was into sex back then. We were just into lowness, like my granny said.

I had one little girlfriend, Martha Gilyard, and her parents didn't believe in whipping kids. I had learned it was a no-no to be in our house during the day. But Grandma was out back, washing clothes, so we went into the house and started playing leapfrog. Well it was my turn to be down on all fours, and as I looked down between my legs to see where Martha was, I saw a big foot with a boot headed my way.

Papa had left again when Mama was pregnant with me. Now it was 1938, and he just got back and came into the house from his latest "absence" and saw kids in the house. He didn't even know it was his kid he kicked. He just kicked me so hard it sent me all the way across the room. Then he snatched us both up and beat our behinds.

That was the first time I had ever seen my daddy. I was three years old.

My daddy wasn't a nice person. He'd get Mama pregnant and then he'd leave for years at a time sometimes, and her and Grandma did the best they could 'til he came back. What we found out after he died was he had two other wives with kids he could go to when he left us.

I was eleven when my father left my mom with nine kids and a sick mother. But I was glad he left. It was harder for us moneywise, but we didn't have to worry about getting beat all the time.

One time some guys were selling big Stone Mountain watermelons near our house. We didn't have any money, and there weren't any restaurants near there. So we traded our whole bowl of macaroni and cheese for a watermelon. It took two of us to tote. Then we had to go back after they left and tear the bushes up around there looking for the bowl. Mama didn't have many dishes or pots, because Daddy had burned our house down. That's when we were living in the unfinished house in Daytona Beach while we were building it (us kids and the boarders).

And then I got married in 1951, got divorced, and came back home in 1952. I stayed home until 1955, when I married Jack Deen. And now we've been together fifty-six years.

*   *   *

All in all, I think I got grown up pretty good. Living is like driving. It isn't a right; it's a privilege. And every morning I wake up and don't smell smoke or hear angel wings flapping, I consider myself lucky. And it makes me happy during the day when I think about it. And when I think about it, I just start singing.

*   *   *

I went to my father's funeral when I was thirty-five. He died of a heart attack in the hospital. He had a sunstroke on the street, and the doctor wanted him to stay in the hospital. He grabbed the doctor by the throat and was choking him. If he hadn't had the heart attack, he likely would have killed the doctor.

Granny said Papa was not a bad man; he just had a bad spirit in him. We were getting ready for his funeral, and she told me I should put garlic in his coffin so the bad spirit couldn't get out and get in someone else at the funeral. But she forgot to say how much. So my sister June and I bought a pound, and we asked the funeral people if we could be the last to see the body before they closed the casket. We put the whole pound in there with him. That spirit went into the ground!

Memories of June

When we were kids, I was always jealous of my little sister June. She was a small, petite little girl—a perfect little angel—kind of like Shirley Temple. I was always gangly and bigger than my brothers and sisters.

June had pale blond hair that Mama or Grandma tied up with rags to make ringlets. She was small and very cute, and everyone loved her. She always got a lot of attention when we went anywhere, which wasn't too bad for the rest of us, because June usually shared the candy or cookies people gave her.

One of my earliest memories of June is when our brother, Raymond, who would babysit us, would take us out to find firewood for our grandma, who cooked on a woodstove. Raymond had a wagon made of a sheet of plywood, four feet by eight feet, with four car tires as wheels. We could go all over the woods and cow pastures near our home in Allendale. June, Zane, Malcolm, and I sat on the wagon. Usually Malcolm held onto the rope that guided the wagon, and Raymond ran behind us, pushing.

Sometimes my older sisters and brothers would to take us down to the river. The little kids seldom went in. They tied us to a tree near the edge of the river, so we could get our feet wet and splash—not deep enough to drown.

This particular day was in 1941, I believe. I was six; June was three. We were walking through the woods when suddenly, June pulled her little panties off. She would squat like she was going to pee, then get up and run a few steps, and then squat down again. It was an odd thing for her to do, because she was always persnickety about her little underwear. So we all ran over to her. Lorraine got there first, grabbed her under her arms, and slung her high into the air. Then the rest of us got up there.

June had been trying to get a rattlesnake to sit still while she peed on him. He kept backing up and coiling and backing up and coiling, and she kept trying to catch him! Robert and Frank had to kill the snake.

Not long after that, my grandma had to go back to Charleston, South Carolina, for something. School was starting, and we had

Michael A Davis

no one to leave June with. So my father said I was to take June to school with me. I was six and in the first grade. So she went. She sat on the floor by my desk and learned everything I did.

June was left-handed, and in those days, they tied your left hand behind you to make you use your right hand. But it didn't work with June, and our father made them quit that little habit.

We had a red rooster who used to chase June every time she went out of the house. She would run and holler. My daddy wanted to keep the rooster, but my grandma said the next time she had to quit what she was doing to chase that red rooster, his days were up. We didn't really think she meant it, because Daddy made this big speech about keeping him.

Later than afternoon, June started screaming again. The red rooster had her backed up to the woodpile, and he was pecking at her. Grandma got behind him, grabbed him by the neck, snapped it, and we had chicken and rice for supper. Daddy didn't realize it 'til after supper, when he saw the pinfeathers in a bag on the clothesline. My grandma made pillows out of pinfeathers off all the chickens she killed.

Our daddy had a neat way of finding out what kind of lowness we had been up to. He paid you a nickel to tell on someone and then at night, while you were asleep, he took the nickel back. Well one time I told on Malcolm for something, Daddy gave me a nickel, and he whipped Malcolm for what I had told on him for. Then he whipped me for telling on Malcolm. So I made up my mind he wasn't getting that nickel back.

So the next day, my best friend, Martha, and I tried everything we knew to get out of taking June to the store with us. You could get ten candy kisses or ten Mary Janes for a penny. Martha and I were going to get fifty pieces of candy and eat it all. But we couldn't get away from June. So we were running down the highway. It wasn't smooth asphalt like we have nowadays—it was mostly sandy and rocky and bumpy.

Well June was running after us, and she tripped and fell. She cut herself right between the eyes, and it knocked her unconscious. We thought she was dead. We were going to carry her down and throw her in the river! But when we went by the post office, the lady there made us bring her inside. We didn't know dead people don't bleed.

Anyway, June came to, and I had to give her the nickel and walk her to the store. She bought Mary Janes and peppermint sticks and didn't give me or Martha not one piece! And then we got in trouble for letting her get hurt. She had the scar all her life.

When we were children, if someone in your family got a childhood disease—measles, chicken pox, mumps, or whooping cough—they quarantined your house. Nobody went to work or to the store. Everyone stayed inside 'til nobody had a fever anymore. They put a big red sign on your front door. Of course I caught everything, and the four of us had to stay in for two months, 'til everyone was over it.

Mama and Daddy were off working when we got quarantined, so they couldn't come back in all this time. But when they did come back, they brought gifts for June, their baby. Me and Malcolm and Zane were excluded from their reunion with their baby. We had been sick, but Daddy put June in his lap and rocked her and sang, "She's my curly-headed baby," and acted like she was the only kid in the room.

We were mad and jealous, but it wasn't June's fault. It was our parents'. They could have patted us on the head to let us know they were sorry. We were sick, too.

Papa took off in the spring of 1945, and not too much happened in our lives over the next year and a half. We kids were glad. We didn't know what could happen to us.

We worked on getting the Harrison Road house built in Daytona Beach. It was almost exactly across the river from our Peninsular Drive house that Papa burned down before he took off finally and for good. But there was no bridge back then, so you had to drive to Daytona, cross the bridge, and drive back down to Harrison Road. We camped in the shell of the house while we were building it.

Mama had bought these lots during the Depression for two or three dollars tax money.[4]

We had that big old pile of used bricks Daddy had gotten for free when they tore down the old school in Port Orange. So Malcolm, Zane, June, and I cleaned the cement off these old, different-colored bricks, and we used them to build our new house in Daytona. By now, our mother had nine children at home and a sick mother.

One time June and her friend, Sandra Hevey, talked me into helping buy a pack of cigarettes—Lucky Strikes—for twenty cents. June walked right by Mama that night, but when I started

---

[4]   In Florida at that time, they would sell off tax certificates on your property if you hadn't paid your taxes within a certain time; I think it was three years. So you could buy a piece of land for the price of the tax certificate. Back then it was just a few dollars.

by, she pointed her finger at me and said, "You have been smoking!" I was eleven years old.

She didn't whip me, but I had to go to town with her the next day, and every time she looked at me, I was to say, "I will not smoke." Stores in Daytona were all over town, not all together like malls today. If she looked at me and I wasn't paying attention, she would slap my face in front of everyone. From that day, if anyone even offered me a cigarette, I would knock them silly. I never smoked. But June did.

From then on, if Mama told me, "You will not" do something, I never did. That was a forever promise.

June would frequently talk me into things and then see how it would turn out. If not much trouble happened to me, she would do it, too. No one usually said anything to her. She was just following my bad example. She talked me into shaving my legs—we wore dresses six inches below our knees, so no one would have known, but she had to tell it. So the next week she started shaving hers. June was thirteen; I was fifteen.

Mama got sick about this time. Granny was in a nursing home in Deland. So Lorraine, who was married, took June with her to Pennsylvania, where her husband, George Lee, came from. They stayed there nine months.

Because Mama was too sick to care for Malcolm, Zane, and me, we were sent away. Malcolm and Zane to Marianna Reform School and me to Ocala Girls School for Delinquents. We hadn't done anything wrong, but they didn't have available places in orphanages at the time. Then some men came along who wanted Mama to give them the house. They were going to tear it down, because it was taking too long to finish. But she wouldn't. Instead, she started taking in boarders, and they helped finish the house. Nine months later, in 1949, we were all back together in a finished house with three bedrooms downstairs and six upstairs.

Me and Junie would help fix and serve breakfast. We would give the boarders a half-cup of coffee and then charge them a nickel for more. One of them brought June a box of chocolate-covered cherries every Friday. That was "the" candy in those days. So us kids would play penny-ante poker with the candy at night. Mama worked from two in the afternoon 'til two in the morning, seven days a week. She made salads and rolls at a rich men's club in Daytona and San Remo, where doctors and attorneys went to "unwind."

When I went to school parties, I had to take June, and she always managed to embarrass me. At swimming parties, she would tell if I was having my period. In those days, you couldn't go in the water during "that time of the month." One time we went on a hayride, and she managed to pee in the hay and get everyone's clothes wet. And when we got to a bathroom, she said she didn't have to pee. I could have killed her on the spot. Everyone who got their clothes wet knew why!

Then Mama started her in dance lessons, tap and ballet. I had to take her on my bike up there and stay and watch her and bring her home. So I learned everything she did. And I helped her practice. I knew the same dance steps she knew, but when anyone came to visit us, Mama always got June to dance for them.

June and I saved our money and bought a used piano for $45 that we made selling newspapers. The lady who sold it to us gave us piano lessons. So we both learned to play the piano. I could play better than June, because I practiced more, but when Mama's friends came over, I was never asked to play. Just June.

A few years later, June started getting invited to parties herself. She learned to skate. I was always afraid to go faster than I could see. I didn't wear glasses, and I couldn't see much out of my right eye—the one my daddy smacked.

June not only learned to skate, she eventually married the skating teacher and went on to own a skating rink. But she was always beautiful and always a lady. She was never sick, never went to doctors, and then one day she had a brain hemorrhage and died. She was just thirty-eight years old.

June was a good mother and a good friend. Always there if you needed her. Loyal to all her friends—and she had many. Truly a great person.

Michael A Davis

The Memorable Men in My Life

I guess this is the part in everyone's life that most people want to know about—the most memorable men in my life, not counting my husband or father. There have been four, actually.

The first one was a hunchback man named Mr. Coon. I never knew what his first name was. He was our first boarder back in the '40s. He was a carpenter by trade, and he had a lazy, no-good son, Amos, as a helper.

Mama got them to finish the house on Harrison Road after Daddy left. They put a huge roof on the house with four dormer windows that made the rooms bigger. But it was hard times, and we had no actual money, so Mama let Mr. Coon and his son, Amos, board with us, and they worked their regular jobs during the week and worked on our house on weekends.

I always had the feeling that Mr. Coon like Mama, but he was a gentleman of the old school, and Mama was still married to Daddy, so it wouldn't have been proper to say anything of a romantic nature to her.

But he brought June (my sister) chocolate-covered cherries every payday.

And then There Was Matt (1948–49)

Matt Doherty. My grandma Thompson always told us, "Two kinds of men to stay away from—Yankees and sailors." Matt was both.

Mama wanted to start a boardinghouse. We had a large house—nine bedrooms—so money being short after Daddy left, we started a boardinghouse. One of my brothers met Matt at work. They worked at a frozen food place. They loaded and unloaded the trucks. It was very hot one day, and my brother Malcolm didn't have any lunch. So he went into the freezer to get something to eat, and the door accidentally locked after him. When Matt went into the freezer after lunch, Malcolm was squatting by the door, nearly frozen to death. He was in pretty bad shape.

So their boss asked Matt to take him home. And that's how we met Matt.

I decided he belonged to me—after all, I saw him first. But that's not the way it goes. He told me he was too old for me. At the time I was twelve, and he was eighteen. I thought he meant "old," like maybe thirty.

So here I am—twelve—and he's patting me on the head, telling me I was a good kid. And until the last time I saw him, he was still doing it.

He was an actual boyfriend to my two older sisters at different times. And we remained friends as long as I knew him. When I was forty-two, I went to Philadelphia to his home. I took my youngest son. We spent three days up there. He thought we ate a lot, so he loaded up with food. The first night we were there, his sister took us out to a nice restaurant. I had chicken; my son, Daniel, got ribs.

Now these folks were eating with knives and forks. I saw that Daniel was having a problem figuring what to use where. So I traded plates with him. And then I just picked up those ribs and ate them with my fingers.

Everyone at our table starred at me a minute and then picked up their fried chicken and BBQ ribs and ate with their fingers!

And I Will Never Forget Sergeant Witt (1947)

Sergeant Witt came into our life when our life was in pretty good shape, when they put the rehab hospital in Daytona for men recovering from the war. I believe it was called the Mary Karl Rehab Center.[5] Our mother got a job there as a nurse's aide and made steady money. One day they admitted a man who

---

[5]   Mrs. Karl was a commercial teacher for the Daytona Beach School System when she was named director of the Opportunity School in 1937. During her tenure, she broadened the training programs offered by the school into areas such as automobile mechanics and body repair, aircraft mechanics, beauty culture, horticulture, welding, and boat building. In order to secure more property for her growing school, Mrs. Karl in 1948 was able to persuade the War Assets Administration to donate to the school system federally owned land on what today is International Speedway Boulevard, known then as the Welch Center and used as an army convalescent home and rehabilitation center. The Opportunity School eventually evolved in to the Mary Karl Vocational School, which later became the technical division of Daytona Beach Junior

had been in the Battle of the Bulge. He was in shock. He was unconscious when he first came in, though we didn't know at the time.

His wife's name was Verge, and Mama's was Virginia. When he came to, he spotted Mama and insisted she was his wife. He was a very large man and out of his head from the battle he had been in. So to calm him down, the doctors agreed to let him come live at our house. It was, after all, a boardinghouse.

Mama worked at the hospital all day, so we got to spend all day, every day, with Sergeant Witt. He ran our house like he ran the army. If we didn't jump to when he told us something, he would slap his fist into his other hand and say, "I'm going to lower the boom on you kids."

Every day he gave us a note, and we walked to the liquor store, and we all got a fifth of whiskey apiece. Sergeant Witt drank whiskey like water. But it took a lot to get him down. We had a little white dog we called Lady because of the slow, careful way she ate her food. When Sergeant Witt tried to get too close to Mama, Lady would get between them.

We lived one-half block from the ocean. Every night Sergeant Witt would swim straight out into the water until we couldn't see him and then swim back in. One day in hurricane season, he did that, and the current took him down the beach a couple of miles before he could get back to shore.

In the meantime, Mama called the Coast Guard. We went all up and down the beach, looking for him. I cut my foot and had to go home. When I got to the paved road, I saw a line of cars coming my way, but something seemed to be holding them up. It was Sergeant Witt. He was walking straight down the road, hollerin' and cussin' with every breath. I went and got him and took him home. But he would only go to the driveway. He wouldn't go in the house, because Mama wasn't there. So I had to go back to the beach to get her.

One day his wife came to see him. She hated Mama instantly. So we hated her instantly. She eventually took him home to New Bern, North Carolina. Every once in a while, he would run away from home and come to us in Daytona. He had been an umpire in baseball in New Bern.

It has been a long time since we've heard from him. But every time we have boiled shrimp, I think of him. When he stayed with us, he once bought ten pounds, and Mama boiled them. She asked him if he had ever eaten them before. "Of course," he said. Then he started eating them, shells and all. So Mama had to peel his. He had only eaten fried or already peeled shrimp before.

And Finally, There Was the Mailman

Great-Uncle William Howard—Grandma Elizabeth's brother.

Ten years after the Civil War, he got the opportunity to develop new land in Florida. Because the Seminole Indians were the only tribe of Indians who never gave up, most of Florida belonged to them. So my great-uncle got a land grant.

This is how it worked. You were to put stones at the four corners of whatever land you intended to claim and make improvements on it. And the other thing you had to do was not leave the land for more than thirty days for seven years.

Great-Uncle William got his grant on what is known today as Merritt Island, or Cape Canaveral Space Coast. It really is an island. He had an agreement with the federal government to deliver mail from Titusville north to Cocoa to the south. Every day he walked the coast along his island. It was about a twenty-mile walk.

That wasn't easy in those days, because the mosquitoes were really out of control. William was alone on the island except for the Indians, who thought he was crazy, and an occasional person looking for land of their own.

William made a home, put in his fences, had a few pigs and chickens, and made a large rain barrel to catch rainwater for drinking and various household chores. But the rain barrel came to be his downfall, because it collected mosquito eggs. Believe it or not, after six years and nine months, William came down with a fever.

The Indians found him awful sick and took him to Titusville, where people not knowing who he was kept him until he died.

By the time his family found out about him, he had lost his claim to his land, and it was given to someone else.

Many stories have been passed down by different people in that area who had the chance to meet the barefoot mailman from Merritt Island . . . my great-uncle William Howard.

My Granny

I remember being raised mostly by my grandma. Her name was Frances Elizabeth Thompson but everyone around those parts called her "Old Miss." Except we kids called her Grandma or Granny. She was a wise and wonderful person. She never had to hunt for anything. If you asked her for something, she had these huge pockets on her apron, and in those pockets were needles, thread, scissors, paper, pencils, nail clippers, tweezers. Anything at all. And always quilt scraps. In case she had to wait anywhere. "Idle hands are the devil's tools." That's what she always said.

I remember walking to town to get groceries with her. I wasn't alone; we had eleven children in our family, and most of us went to town when our granny went. It was like an honor of sorts just to get to walk with her. I was proud to let everyone know she was my grandma.

The store, which seemed a long way at the time, was probably four or five miles from our home. But my grandma bought five—and ten-pound packs of things, so it wasn't a big chore. She bought beans, rice, sugar, meal, grits, and a little coffee. She was partial to a little coffee in the mornings.

When we got to the store, we kids never went in. We all had about six to eight feet of light rope around our waists. We put this on every time we went to town, and with this, my granny would tie us to a post or someone's car bumper 'til she was ready to walk home. She was never gone for very long. Then we each would be given a package to tote home. The packages got moved around when you got tired of toting one.

Our ropes were tied together on the way home, so if we got tired, someone would notice, and the package could be given to someone else for a while. But like I said, going with Granny to the store was a big honor, and we carried our packages honorably.

My grandma cooked twelve quarts of beans and eight quarts of rice a day. And always a pan of biscuits or cornbread. My father did not believe in children eating meat, so we didn't get any. But on Sunday, Granny made a huge macaroni and cheese dish. And we had a cow, so we had plenty of milk and butter.

My grandma was the only doctor anyone knew about in those days. So she gathered roots and moss plants and herbs for people who came to her to be cured. She said the oldest girl in her family was always the doctor. But as things were getting "modern" like they were, my mother chose to go to a doctor in town. And he would come to visit you—on a bicycle. But us kids never saw a doctor 'til most of us were grown. My granny doctored us with preventive medicine. She gave us medicine before we got sick, so we didn't get sick like other kids.

My grandma had a long coin purse. It was like the ones people today put cigarettes in. But it was real leather and soft. She kept it pinned in her "bosom." In her day there were no bras, and ladies bound their breasts down so they looked flat-chested. But she kept her coin purse in there. If anyone was foolish enough to ask her for money, she would only lend a nickel at a time. But in those days, a nickel could easily be worth $20 today. She always had a saying about lending: "Don't lend more than you can afford to lose, because when you lend it, it's gone. Don't sit around worrying about getting it back. If you do get it back, thank God for your good fortune, but if you don't, don't hate the person you lent it to. Be glad you were able to help someone."

She always told us, "Make a circle. You do something for someone, don't ask that he do something for you; let him help someone else. And ask that the circle continue."

I have never met anyone like my granny. She never had one day in school. She couldn't read or write. She unselfishly doctored other people—usually for nothing. She took care of all us kids so my mom could work when our dad ran off to be with another woman, leaving my mom with nine children, all too young to work.

My granny made our clothes, our blankets, and took care of the house. This was in the time before electric lights. She boiled our clothes in the yard in a big pot. She made soap and knew how to get nine kids home from school every day without scolding or threats. She made a big pan of "sweeten bread"; when I got grown, I found out that's cake. Sometimes she made "fried sweeten bread"; I found out later that's donuts.

I never knew my granny to raise her voice or use any curse words. She never said damn—dern—doggone. Nothing. Calmest person I ever knew. On Saturday she walked to town with us.

When we were older, she walked us to the movies. And we walked her to town on Sunday for church.

She never turned anyone away from our house who was hungry. She would just put more water in the beans and smile.

She made our mattresses out of moss from trees. She'd make a fire in the yard, put a piece of tin over it, heat the moss to kill all the red bugs and other bugs, and put it in heavy cloth we called "ticks." All the kids had a spoon tied around their neck with mason cord. Our chairs and plates were hung on the wall.

Child Abuse?

Everything you hear about today is child abuse. When we were children, no one even knew those words, or if we ever heard them, we didn't know what they meant.

We lived in the country—way out in the country. And we thought we were brought up royally. But now that I am grown, I realize our childhood would be laughed about today. But we all lived, and we all knew right from wrong. And we all knew God, and we had respect for our elders.

My grandma didn't believe in sitting around the house during the day. In fact, we were not allowed back into the house after breakfast until supper. If you did mess up and come back, you better be sick. It really wasn't a good idea, because if you came back, you either got doctored or you had to work around the house. There was always work to do around the house. So we learned to stay outside. Mostly. We always found our lunch in the woods—berries or palmetto hearts—wild fruit. There was always something.

My grandma had a radio you could listen to. It ran on a battery. She only listened to the news; her brother, my uncle, was in the army. Once in a while, she let us listen to the Grand Ole Opry in Nashville on Saturday nights.

We turned out all right.

But when I hear all this talk about child abuse today, it just makes me wonder, What **are** they talking about?

Amelia's Poems

(Written through the years, many times
after seeing my mother crying in her room.)

As I sit here, my mind goes far
Down the driveway past the car.
Oh how my mind does wander far.

But I sit here and dream my dreams,
For all of them are beyond my means.
My children come in, laughing and gay,
Say to me, "Mom, please don't stray."

So I sit here, and let my mind go far
Down the driveway past the car . . .
For my children I will stay,
And dream away another day.

*   *   *

To see hatred come and go,
Yet every day steadily grow.
To cuss and rave about nothing,
Then sit here and turn this ring.
I have a hatred yet unbred.
It won't be gone until I'm dead.
So here I am, with you here,
And dread to even have you near.
Would fate deal me such a low blow?
'Til then, only time and I will know.

*   *   *

I have a child who fills my heart
with pleasure.
For all the world, her love I could
not measure,
As she has been my heart's delight.
She fills my heart with song these
bitter nights,
For she remembers, as I do, our friend,
Who time and distance cannot mend.
All fond memories are now of then,
For this is all we have left of him.

*   *   *

Christmas comes again this year.
But now I have no time for cheer,
As anger and unhappiness linger here.
How can you fill your heart with cheer?
Let the bells ring loud to say,
"Oh let me have one happy day."

*   *   *

My ring is gold.
My eyes are blue.
He said he loved me.
I believed him, too.
My ring's still gold.
My eyes still blue.
Why couldn't he still love me, too?

*   *   *

"Don't wait for me, I won't be back.
I'm moving on down the track."
I'll be here, sad and lonely,
Waiting for you, darling, only.
Maybe you don't love me now.
I'll wait for you for a while.
As times change, you'll come to me
And ask me back.
Wait and see.

*   *   *

If I could have one wish,
Tonight I couldn't make a choice,
For I have my dreams unfulfilled.
I know not where to start.
If I could settle on just one thing,
I guess it would say
To have one quiet peaceful day.

*   *   *

Michael A Davis

Smiling as the sun comes up
To warm the pretty buttercups,
I see a face so close to my own,
A lover like no one has known.
He waits for me here near the gate.
He knows I'll come.
I won't be late.

*   *   *

To start my life over,
To make the same mistakes,
Some folks would give a fortune.
For me, once is enough.

*   *   *

Don't write to me, he wrote,
I'm married to my darling Evelyn.
Sorrowfully I took his note.
With tears on my face, I wrote,
What does he think of me,
My lover, this man of mine?
I've loved him for most a year.
I want to be forever near.
His love for me did never tarry.
It wasn't me today he married.

*   *   *

A book I need to write
To keep my tears from flowing,
So the world won't be knowing
That my heart is broken
And can never be mended,
As my story has now ended.

*   *   *

Once upon a hilltop
I did sit and dream.
I spent my time with daffodils and such.
Never thought of the now world much.
Waste my precious time on schemes.
All the while the world spins on
And leaves me here among my dreams.

* * *

Ode to a Heartache

My darling, how I long for you.
Of yesterday when the world was new,
When I had you and you had me.
Oh, how peaceful the world could be.

When I remember your touch,
I long to hold you so much.
Do you ever, ever think of me?
Why, why did you set me free???

* * *

My small boy climbs up in the tree
And stares down, shouting at you and me,
As if to say for all to hear,
I love the world, when you are near.

* * *

Take me to the far country,
The land of snow,
For I have dreamed great dreams
I want the world to know.
I want to call from a high mountain.
Take me to see nature's fountains.
Let me live near God for a while.
Then look at my contented smile.

* * *

Michael A Davis

If today I die,
Who would remember?
Who for me would cry?
Would anyone remember?
I think of this and sigh,
For I do not want to die
Unremembered.

*   *   *

A light burns calmly in the distance.
Is someone watching for a lover?
Or is someone on a mercy mission?
All these thoughts I think of now,
And pray it is no one in our town.
Who needs that light in yonder distance,
Except the lover who rushes even now?

*   *   *

A lonely bum walks down the street
And thinks now of his woman, so sweet,
Who he did leave so long ago
And started out searching in this land of woe.
His sweetheart did long ago wed.
As for him, his mind is dead,
For he did leave her oh so long ago,
To search for gold in this land of woe.

*   *   *

While driving on a turnpike,
A big truck lumbered past,
But ran into a small foreign car.
It was an awful crash.

There was dead and dying,
Lying all over the ground.
I tried not to think of my lover
As I read this morning's paper
And see his name and picture there.

Oh Lord, I cry, don't let it be,
For he is the only one who ever really
loved me.

Now I'm alone, as lonely as can be,
For no one knows God has taken
My reason to live from me.

*   *   *

My child whispers softly to me;
I do not answer.
Jesus hears, but he does not answer.
My child calls anxiously to me;
I do not answer.
Jesus hears my child,
But he does not answer.

My child cries for me in deep despair;
I do not answer.
Jesus hears my child and answers . . .
He cries no more.

*   *   *

Our child came in the night
And asks, Mommy can you hear?
Can I lay down by you?
With you, I know no fear,
For in my dreams I dream
Of things, I know not what they mean.
Mommy, can I sleep with you?
Let your love hold me near.
Now my child with Jesus sleeps.
I still hear him, oh my dear.

*   *   *

Michael A Davis

The clock has struck.
The hour is late.
The time has come
To face my fate.
The hangman comes
For me, oh dear.
Help me, O God,
To hide my fear.

* * *

Autumn sunshine, I remember
Leaves of gold and some of amber.
Bring back my love of yesteryear.
Take me there, or bring him here.
For I have longed so for his touch.
I need and want his love so much.

* * *

On the nights I can't go to sleep,
It does no good to count those sheep.
I think of our glorious days.
It has been a long winter since early May,
When our love was young and tender.

Now I cry for our ideals and surrender,
For love is gone, I know not where.
If I did know, I would go there.
Oh Lord, on nights like these I cannot sleep.
Nor can I just rest and count the sheep.

* * *

I never had a babe so dear,
To be so close and yet not near.
I lie and dream of days of peace.
Of them I know so little,
For anger and vengeance stalk my days.
But for me I go where I may,
As anger and vengeance stalk me.
Come with me to a peaceful place,
Where all the good folks know my face.
Let anger and vengeance stalk me.

*   *   *

My love flowers bloom so yellow,
Recalls of memories so mellow.
For I now live in the past
And live each day as if the last.
As my life ended one year ago today,
When my love was called away.

*   *   *

My daughter is a naughty girl,
As all the world's her playroom.
Oh but to see her smile,
I think I'd walk one hundred miles.

*   *   *

Michael A Davis

Thanksgiving Day is past and dear.
I know how vengeful it has been here,
For all is not well in our house.
And never shall peace reign here,
For love and justice are no longer near.
My love has died so long ago,
And never another shall I know.
So another year has passed;
I pray this shall be my last.
For on I grieve in sorrow here,
As has passed another year.

*   *   *

To dream of fame and fortune
Has never been my goal.
To live in peace, contented,
I'd gladly give my soul.
To each his own, I heard some say,
But mine is for one happy day.

*   *   *

I have never in my life
Seen a home so full of strife.
I think of many things to say,
But just look at how we waste the days.
When I look back on my life,
Oh what toll, bad luck, and strife.

8

A Bit of History

Insert Pic/Page – 8 – 1935 Hurricane – Last Train – 1 of 7
Insert Pic/Page – 8 – 1935 Hurricane – Last Train – 2 of 7
Insert Pic/Page – 8 – 1935 Hurricane – Last Train – 3 of 7
Insert Pic/Page – 8 – 1935 Hurricane – Last Train – 4 of 7
Insert Pic/Page – 8 – 1935 Hurricane – Last Train – 5 of 7
Insert Pic/Page – 8 – 1935 Hurricane – Last Train – 6 of 7
Insert Pic/Page – 8 – 1935 Hurricane – Last Train – 7 of 7

A Bit of Parsons History

(Mama's Brothers and Sister)

*F*red Parsons was born January 4, 1904, in Cumberland County, Tennessee. He married Bonnie Palk on February 25, 1928. She died or they divorced, and he married Hattie Mae Norris in 1940. Hattie was born September 8, 1922.

Fred had four children that I know of: a daughter; a son, James Earl Parsons, born in 1929; and a third child, a boy, R. C., who was born in 1943 and died two years later. Son Fred Jr. was born in 1953. He married Glenda Marie Norris in 1971.

Fred Sr. died in Crossville, Tennessee, in November 1983; Hattie died in February 1995. They are buried, along with son R. C., in Creston Cemetery, Cumberland, Tennessee.

Fred Parson grave marker

Carson Parsons was born June 29, 1906, in Cumberland, Tennessee. He married fifteen-year-old Agnes Farris in 1927. Carson owned and farmed land next to his parents in Cumberland County, Tennessee. He and Agnes had two children: Marie, born in 1927, and Carson Jr., born in 1929.

During World War II, Carson served in the navy from March of 1944 until March of 1945. Agnes died in 1962, and Carson moved to Florida and got married again. He died August 27, 1995, in Jacksonville, Florida. He and his second wife, Vivian, are buried in Dinsmore Community Cemetery, Duval, Florida.

Carson Jr. fought in the Korean conflict and obtained the rank of sergeant first class before he was killed in hostile action on January 3, 1951, in Korea. Sadly, he remains MIA.

*   *   *

Carson was my favorite uncle. He had a great personality and was always laughing and cutting up. I only got to see him five or six times in my life, but I do remember his visit in 1968.

He came to see us at the Nebraska house right after his wife died (she had diabetes). He had already moved to Florida, and he brought a woman with him. She seemed very nice. They stayed about a week and then drove back to Florida. The next day, Momma was cleaning up, washing clothes, etc., and when she went to her closet, most of her clothes were gone. Come to find out, the woman was a hitchhiker Carson had picked up on the way, and she stole my mother's clothes when they left.

We sure had a string of bad luck back then!

—Stanley Davis, October 2011

Insert Pic – 8 – Carson (age 68) & Fred (Age 76) Parsons, 1975.jpg

Carson Parsons   **Vivian C. Parsons**
29 Jun 1906–07   May 1930–
27 Aug 1995

Homer Parsons was born in 1909 in Cumberland County, Tennessee. He married Mary Lou Robinson on May 4, 1927. She was born in Tennessee in 1908. Homer owned and farmed land next to his parents and brother, Carson. Homer and Mary's children, that I know of, were Hubert Ralph, William Arthur, Jerry B., Barbara, and Thomas Troy.

Mary died in September 1980; Homer died two years later. They are buried in Creston Cemetery, Cumberland County, Tennessee, along with three of their children.

Homer Parsons   **Mary Lou Horn**
21 Jul 1909–   17 Aug 1908–
31 Mar 1982   21 Sep 1980

Hubert L. "Ralph"   Sherrie M.
11 Jul 1939 – 13 Jul 1985   30 Jun 1960 —

Thomas T. Parsons   Evelyn Marie Whittaker
15 Aug 1932 – 11 Nov 2005   08 Apr 1933 –

William Arthur Parsons
Apr 3 1935–
June 8 1991

OBITUARY—Thomas Troy Parsons—
Crossville Chronicle,
July 3, 2006

Son of Homer Parsons

Thomas Troy Parsons, 73, of Crossville, passed away Nov. 11, 2005. Funeral services were conducted Nov. 13 from the chapel of Crossville Memorial Funeral Home, with Bro. Dillard Cantrell officiating and special music by Dale Robbins and Bucky Hall. Burial was in Creston Cemetery.

Mr. Parsons was born Aug. 15, 1932 in Crossville, the son of Homer and Mary Jo Parsons. He was a member of Bowman Bible Baptist Church and was a boat dock manager at Fairfield Glade before retiring.

Survivors include his wife, Evelyn Whittaker Parsons; sons and daughters-in-law, Troy and Linda Parsons, Larry and Mary Parsons, and Bruce and Jennifer Parsons; daughters and sons-in-law, Elsie and Dale Robbins and Shirley and Donald Beaty; grandchildren, Robby Parsons, Tony Parsons, Heather Carey, Caleb Parsons, Logan Parsons, Trevor Parsons, Dee Robbins, Dustin Robbins, Whitney Beaty and Britney Beaty; great-grandchildren, Sarah Parsons, Kristoffer Parsons, Jakob Parsons, Seth Parsons, Locklyn Robbins and Kylie Robbins; brother, Jimmy Parsons; and sisters, Betty Hedgecoth, Barbara Elmore, Virginia Blaylock and Judy Parsons.

In addition to his parents, he was preceded in death by his brothers, J. B. Parsons, William Arthur "Ted" Parsons and Hubert "Ralph" Parsons; and special mother-in-law, Elcie Whittaker. Pallbearers were Dustin Robbins, D. C. Robbins, Robby Parsons, Tony Parsons, Ronnie Parsons, Mike Harvel and Carol Roberts.

Honorary pallbearers were Caleb and Logan Parsons.

Crossville Memorial Funeral Home and Crematory, Inc. was in charge of the arrangements.

Hubert Parsons was born October 30, 1911, in Cumberland County, Tennessee. He married Marie Gladys Farris. She was born in 1908 and died in 1964. Hubert died in 1989 in Cumberland County, Tennessee. They are buried in Oak Lawn Cemetery, Pomona, Tennessee.

I know of one child, a son: Raymond E. Parsons, born November 28, 1940, in Crossville, died July 5, 2011, in Livingston, Overton, Tennessee.

Hubert Parsons   Gladys M. Parsons
30 Oct 1911 – 17 Sep 1989   02 Sep 1908 – 27 Dec 1964

Ruby Parsons was born July 9, 1914, in Cumberland County, Tennessee. She married Clarence M. Swallows on February 13, 1937. He was born May 15, 1915, in Putnam County, Tennessee.

Ruby and Clarence lived in and around the Crossville area most of their lives. I know they had at least one son, James Marvin, born in April of 1938. James married Bernese Allene Smith in 1964. He died in 2007.

Ruby died in 1977, and Clarence remarried. He died in 2004 and is buried in Green Acres Memorial Gardens in Cumberland County, Tennessee.

*　　*　　*

I have fond memories of Aunt Ruby; she was a good Christian woman. She always treated us kids well; Mama was pretty close friends with her until she died.

—Stanley Davis, October 2011

Obituary—Crossville Chronicle—
August 13, 2004

Husband of Ruby Parsons

Clarence M. Swallows, May 15, 1915–Aug. 6, 2004

Clarence M. Swallows, 89, of Crossville, passed away Aug. 6, 2004. Funeral services were conducted Aug. 9 from the chapel of Crossville Memorial Funeral Home, with burial in Green Acres Memory Gardens. The Rev. Sandy Shawhan officiated.

Mr. Swallows was born May 15, 1915 in Putnam County, the son of Isaac and Effie Swallows. He was a member of First United Methodist Church. Before retiring, he was employed by Volunteer Electric Cooperative for many years.

Survivors include his wife, Mayme Swallows; son and daughter-in-law, James Marvin and Bernese Swallows; stepdaughter and son-in-law, Peggy Flynn and Ray Harris; granddaughter, Leigh Swallows Peterman; step-granddaughter, Monica Leigh; brother, Clinton Swallows; and sisters, Daisy Holt, Gertha Abner, Bertha Dillon and Myrtle Carter.

In addition to his parents, he was preceded in death by his first wife, Ruby Parsons Swallows; stepson, Robert Ted Flynn; brothers, Haskell and Benton Swallows; and sister, Beulah Boatman.

Pallbearers were Fred Parsons, Bud Steele, David Weismuller, Lloyd Jackson, Hugh Goss and Don Moody.

Honorary pallbearers were VEC employees, Ordon Sevier, Ervia Hamby, Glenn Miller, Betty Moody, Irene Weismuller, Paul Whittenburg, Lyle Williams, Raymond Webb and Glen Blaylock.

Crossville Memorial Funeral Home and Crematory, Inc. was in charge of the arrangements.

Mama's Grandparents (William Madison Parsons and Nancy Jane Morrow)

Great-grandfather *William Madison Parsons* was born in May of 1847 in New River, Allegheny County, North Carolina. When he was just fourteen, he tried to enlist with the 37th Infantry of North Carolina and was sent home a month later for being too young. He did reenlist with the same unit in 1863, serving as bugler for the company. He was mustered on in September of 1864.

In 1866 he married *Nancy Jane Morrow,* by which time he was living in Cumberland County, Tennessee. In addition to Mark (Wilma's father), Nancy and William had eight other children.

Nancy died in 1914. Later that year, sixty-seven-year-old William married *Martha Emory.* She was fifty-five. Sadly, Martha died just ten years later. In 1925 William married for a third time, to Miss Lillie Horn. He was seventy-eight; she was forty-five.

Marriage must have agreed with William; he lived to the ripe old age of ninety-one. He died in 1939 and is buried in Creston Cemetery, Cumberland, Tennessee.

Michael A Davis

William and Nancy's children were:

Elizabeth Parsons (1857–1910) married Richard Julian Taylor (1864–1911), and they had three children:

> George Green Taylor (1895–1980)
> Addie J. Taylor (1897–1993)
> Virgil Taylor (1901–)
> Nora Taylor (circa 1903–)
> Henry Lee (1868–)

Henry Lee Parsons (1858–1953) married Harriett Letitia "Hattie" Pugh (1876–1970) in 1891. They had two children: Grover Cleveland Parsons (1892–1988) and Myrtle Parsons (1895–?).

Henry Lee and Hattie are buried in Creston Cemetery, Cumberland, Tennessee.

HATTIE PARSONS

Mrs. Hattie Lee (Tish) Parsons passed away Wednesday, May 13, at her home on Rt. 1, Crossville, following an extended illness. She was 94. 1967?

Services were conducted Saturday morning at the Baker's Crossroad Freewill Baptist Church with the Rev. H. J. Chadwick officiating. Goff Funeral Home of Monterey was in charge.

Mrs. Parsons leaves a daughter and son Mrs. Myrtle Taylor and Grover Parsons, both of Crossville; seven grandchildren; 25 great-grandchildren; and 21 great-great-grandchildren.

Grandsons serving as pallbearers were Donald, Lowell, Larry and Steve Pugh, Wayne and Lane Madewell, Fred and Ralph Wilson, Gerry and Sammy Bryant, Robert Parsons and Olin North.

Tincy Angeline Parsons (1869–1882). Tincy never married. She is buried in Creston Cemetery, Cumberland, Tennessee, in the Parsons family plot.

Eli Isham "Guff" Parsons (1871–1949) married Effie Jane Smith (1881–1967) in 1902. They had three children: William L., born in 1903; James, born in 1905; and Nancy A., born in 1908.

Guff built the Cumberland Mountain Filling Station and Grocery on Highway 70N, five miles out of Crossville in 1900. Together, Uncle Guff and Aunt Effie ran the store until he died.

Guff and Effie are buried in the Parson family section of Creston Cemetery, Cumberland, Tennessee.

end. *Jan F 1968*

AUNT EFFIE PARSONS

Mrs. Effie Jane Parsons of Bakers Crossroads passed away Dec. 21 at the age of 86. "Aunt Effie," as she was known, came to Tennessee from Wisconsin as a small child and had lived most of her life here.

Funeral services were held Sunday, Dec. 24 at the Bakers Freewill Baptist Church, with the Rev. John Barnes and the Rev. Talmadge Bowman officiating. Burial was in Creston cemetery.

"Aunt Effie" was the wife of the late Guff Parsons. She is survived by two sons, Jim and Willie Lee; one daughter, Nancy Lowe; eight grandchildren and 20 great-grandchildren.

She was a member of the Bakers Freewill Baptist Church.

According to her death certificate, *Amanda Victoria "Manda" Parsons* was born September 17, 1869, but her gravestone says 1872. She first married Augustus Everritt "Duck" Smith in 1890. He was born in Polk, Wisconsin, and registered for service in World War I; however, he was forty-six years old. I presume he did not serve. He and Amanda had seven children:

> Emma Mae (1891–1969)
> Maude Stevens (1892–1977)
> Frances (1897–196)
> William (1899–1929)
> Nancy (1902–1976)
> Ridley M. (1905–1933)
> Venable Lane (1908–1913)

This picture was taken in 1910. The baby, Venable, died of lockjaw in 1913, after stepping on a nail. Duck was building a new home in Crossville when this happened, and when Venable died, Duck just walked away from it and never finished it.[1]

[1]Courtesy Margie Smith Online Ancestry Public Tree.

Amanda and Everett divorced, and she married M. V. "Caney" Henry in 1931. Everett Smith died in 1935; Amanda died in 1947. Caney Henry died in 1956. Amanda and Everett are buried in the Parsons family plot in Creston Cemetery, Cumberland, Tennessee.

NOTE: The Gravestone actually reads:
Mrs. M. V. Henry (1872–1947)

William Madison "Wid" Parsons Jr. was born December 23, 1872, in Cumberland County, Tennessee. In 1898 he married Ota Starnes Elmore. She was born in April 1881. They had six children:

Lester (1898–1981)
Bryan (1899–1967)
Murray (1902–1996)
Roscoe (1904–1997)
Gilbert (1907–2002)
Lina Beecher (1909–1976)

William died in 1950; Ota died in 1959. They are buried in the Parsons family plot in Creston Cemetery, Cumberland, Tennessee, along with several of their children.

William Madison Parsons Jr.   Ota Starnes Elmore
(1873–1950)   (1881–1959)

Mary Jane Parsons was born in 1876 in Cumberland County, Tennessee; I'm not sure when she died. She married Hudson Estes France about 1902. He was born August 19, 1876, and died July 6, 1945. They had four children:

> Lee (1903–1911)
> Nancy Edith (1905–)
> Hudson Estes Jr. (1911–1997)
> Hattie Rhea (1914–1984)

Roxina "Roxy" Parsons (1879–1961) married Robert Lee Geer (1871–1952), and they had five children:

Mable Geer (1897–1976)
Myrtle Pearl Geer (1900–)
Helen Geer (circa 1903–)
Geneva Geer (circa 1907–)
Robert Lee Geer (1909–1975)

Roxina and Robert are buried in Highland Cemetery, White County, Tennessee.

Crab Orchard, Tennessee

Crab Orchard is a city in Cumberland County, Tennessee, United States. The population was 838 at the 2000 census.

The town is situated atop the Cumberland Plateau in a gap amidst the Crab Orchard Mountains, a sub-range of the Cumberland Mountains. This gap has long been frequented by travelers moving back and forth between East Tennessee and Middle Tennessee. Today, both Interstate 40 and U.S. Route 70 pass through Crab Orchard.

Big Rock Mountain (el. 2,703 ft/824 m) rises prominently to the north of Crab Orchard. Haley Mountain (el. 2,660 ft/811 m) and Black Mountain (el. 2,827 ft/861 m) dominate the view to the south. A section of the Cumberland Trail will, when completed, traverse Crab Orchard from north to south.

According to the United States Census Bureau, the city has a total area of 11.1 square miles (28.7 km), all land.

History

Crab Orchard's position in a gap in the Crab Orchard Mountains made it an early "gateway" to the Cumberland area as early as the late 18th century. Pioneers passing through the area named it for its abundance of wild crab apple trees.[1] In the 1780s, a road was built through the gap to help provide protection for travelers migrating from East Tennessee to the Nashville area. [5] The historian J.G.M. Ramsey reported several Cherokee, Creek, and Shawano attacks at "the Crab-Orchard" during a period of heightened tensions between Native Americans and encroaching Euro-American settlers in the early 1790s. Around 1792, a small band of troops led by Captain Samuel Handley was attacked by a mixed group of Cherokee, Creek, and Shawano at Crab Orchard, ending in Handley's capture.[2] In April of 1794, a group of travelers was ambushed by a band of Creeks, killing early Cumberland County settler Thomas "Big Foot" Spencer. A few weeks later, a "Lieutenant McClelland" was attacked and routed by a band of Creeks at Crab Orchard.

In the late 18th century, as Cherokee attacks subsided, the Walton Road was built as part of the stage road system connecting the Knoxville and Nashville areas. The road passed through Crab Orchard, bringing a steady stream of travelers and migrants to the area. Around 1800, Sidnor's Inn opened at Crab Orchard, with Bishop Francis Asbury being among its earliest guests. In 1827, Robert Burke, whose wife operated a tavern at what is now Ozone established the Crab Orchard Inn, which would remain open until the early 20th century.

Although one of the oldest communities in the Cumberland area, Crab Orchard was not officially incorporated until 1973.[3]

Stone Quarries and Mines

Crab Orchard has given its name to a rare type of durable sandstone found in its vicinity. First used in local structures and sidewalks in the late 19th century, the Crab Orchard stone gained popularity in the 1920s when it was used in the construction of Scarritt College in Nashville. Numerous buildings in Crossville, including the Cumberland County Courthouse, have been constructed with Crab Orchard stone.[4]

Crab Orchard is also home to a large limestone mine operated by Franklin Industrial Minerals. The mine and its accompanying plant dominate the south side of the Crab Orchard gap along Interstate 40 and US-70.

Franklin Industrial Minerals Mine and Plant, Crab Orchard, TN

References

1. Helen Bullard and Joseph Krechniak, *Cumberland County's First Hundred Years* (Crossville, Tenn.: Centennial Committee, 1956), 122.

2. Ramsey, *Annals of Tennessee,* 571–572.

3. *The WPA Guide to Tennessee* (Knoxville: University of Tennessee Press, 1986), 441. Originally compiled by the Federal Writers' Project of the Works Project Administration as *Tennessee: A Guide to the State,* and published in 1939.

4. Carroll Van West, "Crab Orchard Stone." *The Tennessee Encyclopedia of History and Culture,* 2002. Retrieved: 2 January 2008.

The "Nations," Nashville Neighborhood

The area of West Nashville is known as The Nations. When the old prison was in operation, a lot of family members of the convicts moved to this area as well as guards. People moved from all over and the area attracted a lot of diversity, sparking the nickname, "The Nations."

Along with the majority of close-in sections of Nashville and similar cities nationwide, The Nations underwent a long period of decline when relocation to suburban areas became popular in the 1950s. By the 1980s the area was a haven for crime and drug activity. In recent years The Nations has begun to clean up, with crime rates dropping to city average or below, new infill development, and professional rehabbing of some of the neighborhood's many vintage Craftsman and Victorian homes. The area has benefitted from it's proximity to the fashionable Sylvan Park Neighborhood.

St. Louis, Missouri

They were French and Spanish before they were American. Before European explorers traveled the river, the land was home to the Mississippians, a mighty Indian civilization of mound builders. When that culture disappeared during Europe's Middle Ages, only their mysterious earthen structures remained, earning St. Louis its nickname, "Mound City."

In 1764, French fur traders from New Orleans founded a city named for Louis IX, the Crusader King of France. St. Louis was built in Spanish territory on a high bluff just 18 miles south of the confluence of the Mississippi and Missouri rivers, a perfect site from which to trade with Indians in the fur-rich lands of the west. France regained rights to St. Louis and the west again in the 1800.

When the French began settling in St. Louis, they established a fur trading community. The town developed into a center for north-south commerce along the Mississippi River. St. Louis was closely designed after a French colonial city of the times, probably New Orleans. The early settlement had no retail centers. There were only two granaries, a bakery, a maple sugar works, and a church. Supplies were brought to St. Louis by keelboats with cargoes of flour, sugar, whiskey, blankets, fabrics, tools, and household goods.

The French colonial homes were uniquely structured with wall logs placed vertically and plastered over. Plaster gave the logs a fresh, white exterior. The home typically consisted of a living area, a bedroom, and fireplace in between. The French colonial home was sparsely furnished and may have included straight back wooden chairs, a table, a four poster bed with a buffalo robe spread, and cooking utensils.

Then Napoleon sold the Louisiana Territory to President Thomas Jefferson without taking possession.

When explorers Lewis and Clark set out from St. Louis to chart the Louisiana Territory in 1804, more than 1,000 people, mostly French, Spanish, Indian and black, both free and enslaved, lived in the city which was already the center of the fur trade in America. Two years later, after the explorers returned from the Pacific with their Corps of Discovery, St. Louis became the last stop for pioneers, mountain men, trappers and travelers heading to the frontier. For decades, entrepreneurs would make fortunes selling goods to explorers and trading for furs.

The first steamboat arrived in 1817, heralding a new era of commerce and travel along the Mississippi. Soon it was common to see more than 100 steamboats lining the levee at one time. This was the Mississippi that Mark Twain came to know as a river boat pilot, and later as an author.

In 1849, a deadly fire destroyed a third of the city when the steamboat White Cloud exploded on the river front. It destroyed exactly15 blocks of the center of the city and caused 6.1 million dollars in damage. The Old Courthouse and Old Cathedral were stone structures and not destroyed. St. Louis was built again, this time with brick and iron rather than easily kindled wood.

While Missouri remained with the Union, the Civil War divided St. Louis as it divided the nation. Abolitionists shared the streets with slave holders, and the Dred Scott trials, which began at the Old Courthouse, helped lead the nation toward Civil War after the U.S. Supreme Court verdict that denied citizenship and rights to slaves.

New immigrants changed the face of St. Louis throughout the 19th century. Joining the French, Spanish, Indian and African descendants were Germans who settled in St. Louis and along the Rhine-like Missouri River valley, and Irish immigrants fleeing the famine on their island.

In 1874, the completion of the Eads Bridge across the Mississippi heralded a new day for the Iron Horse. As railroads grew, steamboat traffic declined. St. Louis became a major industrial center with more than 100 breweries operating in the city. Clothing and shoe manufacturers thrived along the Washington Avenue garment district, and St. Louis was known as "first in shoes, first in booze, and last in the American League," a reference to the St. Louis Browns baseball club.

In 1904, the Louisiana Purchase Exposition celebrated the 100th anniversary of the Lewis and Clark expedition. Forest Park became a glittering expanse of palaces and attractions, drawing 20 million visitors and exhibits from 43 countries. Popular foods, including the ice cream cone and iced tea, were invented at the fair. Scott Joplin's new ragtime music enthralled visitors, and the song "Meet Me in St. Louis, Louis" summed up the most glorious time St. Louis had ever seen.

The fair, and the 1904 Olympic Games, which took place at Washington University, defined St. Louis as a world-class city.

The first International Balloon Race was held in St. Louis in 1908, and less than 20 years later Charles Lindbergh captured the imagination of the world by crossing the Atlantic non-stop. His 1927 solo flight from New York to Paris took place in an airplane named Spirit of St. Louis thanks tot he financial backing of St. Louis businessmen. In 1965, the Gateway Arch opened as a monument to the important role St. Louis played in America's westward expansion.

— http://www.univie.ac.at/Anglistik/webprojects/
LiveMiss/stlouis/history.htm.

* * *

St. Louis Arch

The Gateway Arch, or Gateway to the West, is an arch that is the centerpiece of the Jefferson National Expansion Memorial in St. Louis, Missouri. It was built as a monument to the westward expansion of the United States. At 630 feet (192 m), it is the tallest

154   Michael A Davis

man-made monument in the United States, Missouri's tallest accessible building, and the largest architectural structure designed as a weighted or flattened catenary arch.

Located on the west bank of the Mississippi River where the city of St. Louis was founded, the arch was designed by Finnish American architect Eero Saarinen and structural engineer Hannskarl Bandel in 1947. Construction began on February 12, 1963, and ended on October 28, 1965, costing US$13 million at the time ($90,491,005 today). The monument opened to the public on June 10, 1967.

Fathers of Charleston

My father's people came from Charleston. Great-great-grandfather *Enoch Hutson* was born in 1824 in Colleton, South Carolina. He married Sarah Wood about 1843. She was also born in Colleton, in 1828. Enoch and Sarah had three children: my great-grandmother Lavina, Agnes, and Sarah.

In researching this family, I found Enoch and Sarah with their three children living in St. Paul's Parish in 1850: Lavina, age five; Agnes, age three; and baby Sarah. By 1860, however, at the young age of thirty, Sarah was the head of her household, living with her two brothers, William and Rhett Wood, and only two children, Lavina and Agnes. Little Sarah had died. As had Enoch, sometime before his thirty-sixth year. Tragically short lives. They are buried in Ravenel, South Carolina.

Great-Grandmother Lavina E. Hutson was born in 1845 in Colleton and married *Great-Grandfather James Albert Davis* in 1862 in Colleton. He, too, was born in Colleton in 1845. Lavina died in 1910; James had died in 1908. I have been to their gravesites; all are buried in White Church Cemetery, Ravenel, South Carolina.

Great-Grandfather James Albert was barely seventeen when the Civil War started. According to the records I found, he joined the Confederate Army and participated in several battles. I discuss this later in this chapter.

James & Lavina (Hutson) Davis
White Church Cemetery
Ravenel, South Carolina

James
17 Apr 1845 -
24 Oct 1908

Lavina
14 Apr 1845 -
04 Jul 1910

In addition to my grandfather Enoch Nathan, James and Lavina had eleven other children. Four of them did not survive childhood, having died prior to 1880. They were: *Maria A. Davis*, born 1867; *Wesley Davis*, born 1873; *Sarah A. Davis*, born 1874; and *John Benjamin Davis*, born 1875. One son, *Franklin C.* might have been stillborn, having been born and died in 1885.

Bits and Pieces of the
Children Who Survived

James Mikel Davis was born May 26, 1863.

In searching census records, I could never find the adult James. Then I found his death certificate, which may explain why.

I learned a great deal from this record, sad but helpful information. It was issued from the State Hospital for the Insane, located in Columbia, South Carolina, where James had been a resident for sixteen years, ten months, and four days. And then he died on August 29, 1915.

How could this be? Why was he living there?

According to his death record, the primary cause of death was pellagra, with a secondary cause of pulmonary edema. Pellagra? I had no idea what this was, so I looked it up.

I learned that pellagra can develop from a nutritionally poor diet. It is sometimes a side effect of alcoholism, as well.

In the early 1900s, pellagra reached epidemic proportions in the American South. There were 1,306 reported pellagra deaths in South Carolina during the first ten months of 1915; 100,000 Southerners were affected in 1916. At this time, the scientific community held that pellagra was probably caused by a germ or some unknown toxin in corn.

The Spartanburg Pellagra Hospital in Spartanburg, South Carolina, was the nation's first facility dedicated to discovering the cause of pellagra. It was established in 1914 with a special congressional appropriation to the U.S. Public Health Service (PHS)and set up primarily for research.

In 1915, Joseph Goldberger, assigned to study pellagra by the Surgeon General of the United States, showed that pellagra was linked to diet by inducing the disease in prisoners, using the Spartanburg Pellagra Hospital as his clinic. By 1926, Goldberger established that a balanced diet or a small amount of brewer's yeast prevented pellagra.

*   *   *

Both alcoholism and not consuming enough green vegetables, seafood, meat, and eggs commonly cause primary pellagra. Secondary pellagra occurs when sufficient niacin is consumed but not taken up and used by the body. Secondary pellagra is often caused by gastrointestinal diseases that prevent absorption of niacin. Because tryptophan is needed to make niacin, low levels of tryptophan may also lead to pellagra.

The signs and symptoms of pellagra can be constant or occur periodically. Pellagra varies among individuals. Some people with pellagra have mild symptoms, such as fatigue, while others may develop severe depression and anxiety. Fortunately, pellagra can be treated with nutritional supplementation to resolve deficiencies in niacin. Lifestyle changes can reduce your risk for pellagra and include limiting alcohol intake, eating a well-balanced diet, not smoking, and always taking all medications and supplements as prescribed.

In some cases, if left untreated, pellagra can lead to dementia, anxiety or depression that should be immediately evaluated in an emergency setting. Seek immediate medical care (call 911) if you, or someone you are with, have any of these serious symptoms, including altered mental status, alcohol withdrawal, or severe depression with suicidal thoughts.

— http://www.bettermedicine.com/article/pellagra

This is mere conjecture on my part, but I suspect James became an alcoholic early in his adult life. Possibly he had a poor diet as a child. Poor nutrition plus heavy drinking could cause him to develop pellagra, the side effects of which could land you in a mental institution.

There has to be a reason he was there for sixteen years. According to his death certificate, he died at age fifty-two. That means he came to this institution when he was thirty-six years old.

Likely I will never know for sure, but it appears James had a sad and tragic life.

William Albert Davis was born February 12, 1866, in Colleton County, South Carolina. He married Anna "Annie" Platt in 1891, when she was seventeen years old. According to the 1910 census of Dorcester, Anna was the mother of ten children, but only six were living at this time: Joseph Allen, John B., Lucy A., William C. F., Raymond U., and Thomas J.

Anna died in 1912; she was just thirty-eight years old. It's hard to imagine bearing ten children in twenty-one years. It is likely this took a toll on her health and may have contributed to her early demise. William died in February of 1913; he was just forty-seven.

William and Anna are buried in White Church Cemetery, Ravenel, South Carolina.

George Nathan Davis was born in 1876 in Colleton County, South Carolina. He married Eliza Platt in 1898. They had two children: Nathan, born in 1900; Levinia, born in 1904. George was a locomotive fireman. He contracted pulmonary tuberculosis and died May 23, 1915, at the young age of thirty-nine. Sadly, Levinia also contracted tuberculosis and died in 1918; she was just fourteen years old.

George and Levinia are buried in Ridge Baptist Church Cemetery in Summerville, South Carolina. I have not been able to find a burial location for Eliza.

Lilla Victoria Davis was born in 1879. That's all I know for sure.

Alfred Harold "Harry" Davis, tenth child of James and Lavina, was born November 9, 1880. He married Ida Postell in November of 1920, when she was just seventeen. Harry and Ida had six children: Ida Belle, Wilma Levinia, Alfred Harold Jr., Loretta "Lottie," Harry Lee, and one more who is still living and prefers to be unnamed here.

Alfred Sr. was just forty-five years old when he died January 9, 1929. Ida outlived him by twenty-nine years and eventually remarried. Both are buried in the Davis family plot in White Church Cemetery, Ravenel, South Carolina.

Mary Elizabeth Davis was born August 27, 1883, in Colleton, South Carolina. She married James Charles Perry sometime before 1900, and they had two daughters: Eva, born in February of 1900 in Ravenel, and Anna, born about 1903 in Dorchester, South Carolina. We believe James died of emphysema in May of 1902, at the young age of twenty-six, and did not live to see his second daughter, Anna.

By 1910 Mary is married to Elias Platt, and records state they had been married for five years. Mary and Elias had four more children: Sarah Virleatha, born in 1908; Lillian Marie, born in February of 1910; Annie Pearl, born in August of 1912; and Mayme Evon, born in November of 1915. Mary died in Charleston in 1946.

Elias lived until 1970. He was living in Clinton, Connecticut at the time of his death.

Franklin C. Davis. I am sorry to say it appears that Franklin died the same year he was born, 1885.

*   *   *

By 1900 James and Lavina had been married thirty-seven years and were living two houses down from his son, Enoch, my grandfather, and had a thirteen-year-old black servant, James Middleton, employed as a cook living with them.

As for my Confederate soldier Great-Grandfather James Albert Davis, I have learned some interesting things about his participation in this gut-wrenching war that tore families and country asunder.

Civil War Record of James A. Davis

James A. Davis originally enlisted in the Third Cavalry Regiment, Company I, South Carolina, in March 1863. James was just eighteen years old at the time and already married to Lavinia. The men of this unit were from Marlon, Colleton, Beaufort, Barnwell, and Calhoun counties of South Carolina under the command of Colonel Charles J. Colcock.

This unit was assigned to the Department of South Carolina, Georgia, and Florida, and confronted the Federals in various conflicts in South Carolina. Much of the time it did not serve as one command but in detachments of one, two, five, or six companies. One detachment was involved in the defense of Savannah. Later the regiment saw action in the campaign of the Carolinas. It surrendered with the Army of Tennessee.

CSA Third Cavalry Battles I Believe My Great-Grandpa Fought In

—Coosawhatchie, SC (22–23 Oct. 1862)
—Expedition from Fort Pulaski, GA, to Bluffton, SC (04 Jun. 1863)

In December of 1863, James transferred to the Sixth Cavalry Regiment.

South Carolina Sixth Cavalry Regiment, Company F

Organized at the Citadel, Charleston, South Carolina, on June 9, 1862. Mustered into state service as Captain M. B. Humphrey's Company, SC Cavalry and assigned to Aiken's 1st Regiment SC Partisan Rangers. Mustered into Confederate service as Company F, 16th Battalion SC Cavalry July 23, 1862. Redesignated Company F, 6th Regiment SC Cavalry when its parent organization was increased from battalion to regiment.

(Ranks indicated are as of the date the unit mustered in on July 23, 1862, or the date of enlistment, if later.)

Here is his record of his transfer:

PRIVATES:

Davis, J. A., Pvt. (1843–?) Colleton. Enl. Mar. 1863 in Co. I (Rebel Troop), 3rd SC Cavalry. Exchanged for J. O. Willson and trans. to Cadet Rangers Dec. 1, 1863. Deserted into Union lines Charleston Mar. 9, 1865. Took oath of allegiance and released.*

*   *   *

Battles of the 6th Cavalry
The Wilderness, VA (5–6 May 1864)
Spotsylvania Court House, VA (8–21 May 1864)
North Anna, VA (23–26 May 1864)
Cold Harbor, VA (1–3 Jun. 1864)
Petersburg Siege, VA (Jun. 1864)
Vaughan Road (1 Oct. 1864)
Carolinas Campaign, SC (Feb.–Apr. 1865)
Darlington, SC (27 Feb. 1865)
Solomon's Grove (9 Mar. 1865)
Monroe's Crossroads (10 Mar. 1865)

*   *   *

One month later, April 10, 1865, Robert E. Lee officially surrendered to U. S. Grant at Appomattox Court House in Virginia on behalf of the CSA.

When Lee surrendered in early April 1865, he had only eight thousand troops left in his major force, the Army of Northern Virginia. Hundreds of thousands of others had simply gone home or were "absent"; in military language, they "deserted."

By the first week of May 1865, all of the CSA forces east of the Mississippi had surrendered ("Southern History of the War," Edward A. Pollard, 1866, p. 523).

*It is worth noting that "Deserted into Union lines" is misleading. The original, handwritten CSA military records at the State Archives in Columbia, South Carolina, all say the same thing. At the end of the war, all CSA troops were required to surrender to the Union forces and take an oath of allegiance to the US government. If they did not surrender, they just returned and took an oath of allegiance to the United States, their record was then cleared, and they were free to return home. Theirs was a simple choice—take the oath or be subject to arrest and execution as a deserter.

As for my grandfather, *Enoch Nathan Davis*, he was born November 24, 1869, in Ravenel, South Carolina, and died December 17, 1920 in Charleston. Between times, he managed to marry and father seven children. According to the 1900 census, he married Annie Kent in 1896. He was twenty-nine years old; she was just sixteen. Their first child was born in August of 1898.

In 1900 the family was living in St. Andrew's Township, South Carolina, and Grandpa Enoch was working as a fireman. By 1910 the family had moved to Chatham, Georgia, where he owned and farmed his own land. By 1920 they were back in Charleston, and Grandfather Enoch was working in a shipyard.

After Enoch died, Annie remarried a man named Hodge. She died July 13, 1960, in Charleston.

Enoch and Annie are buried in the Davis family section of White Church Cemetery, Ravenel, South Carolina.

In addition to my father, *Robert Benjamin (aka Roy B.)*, they had five more sons and one daughter: William Arthur, William Nathan "Pete" Davis, Albert E. "Jeff," John Lee, Enoch Cleo, and Edna Irene.

Bits and Pieces of Their Lives

William Arthur Davis was born in August 1898 and does not appear with his family in the 1910 census, which means he was less than twelve years old when he died.

William Nathan "Pete" Davis was born on December 28, 1903, in South Carolina. In 1948 he was working as a security guard. He married Dorothy Inez Mitchum in May of 1938. She was born January 24, 1912. They had eight children: Enoch Nathan, Betty, James Olin, Annie Louise, Boyd E., Smart Benjamin, Margaret M., and William M.

Pete was the brother who made the arrangements to take my father's body back to Ravenel, South Carolina, and bury him in the Davis family plot.

Dorothy died March 22, 1960; William died on March 17, 1988. They are buried in Bonneau Baptist Church Cemetery, Berkeley, South Carolina.

William Pete Davis 1950

William Pete Davis 1948

William Nathan Davis 1903-1988

Dorothy Mitch um Davis 192-1960

Albert E. "Jeff" Davis was born July 7, 1905, in Ravenel, South Carolina. He married Myrtle Daniels in 1927. In 1930 Jeff and Myrtle were living next door to brother William in Charleston. At the time, Jeff was working as a laborer on an oyster boat. He died in December of 1969 and is buried in the Davis family section of White Church Cemetery in Ravenel, South Carolina.

John Lee Davis was born January 9, 1910, in Ravenel, South Carolina, the fifth child of Enoch and Annie. He married Margaret Thelma Mitchell. She was born in 1906 and died in 1979. John Lee died in July of 1971. They are buried in White Church Cemetery, Ravenel, South Carolina.

Enoch Cleo Davis had a tragic and short life. He died in infancy in1912 and is buried in the Davis family plot in White Church Cemetery, Ravenel, South Carolina.

Edna Irene Davis—all I could discover about Edna was that she was born about 1915 and married William H. McSwain in February of 1932.

So there you have it. The life and times of my Charleston ancestors . . . the life of times of a rolling stone . . . the man named Robert Benjamin Davis.

I could not close this chapter without including some interesting and fascinating facts I learned about this famous southern city as I searched for my relatives and ancestors.

A Bit of Charleston History

The history of Charleston, South Carolina, is one of the longest and most diverse of any community in the United States, spanning hundreds of years of physical settlement beginning in 1670 through modern times. Located just south of the mid-point of South Carolina's coastline, at the confluence of the Ashley and Cooper rivers, which flow together into the Atlantic Ocean, Charleston Harbor lies between downtown Charleston and the Atlantic Ocean. Charleston's name is derived from Charles Towne, named after King Charles II of England.

By the mid-18th century, Charleston had become a bustling trade center, the hub of the Atlantic trade for the southern colonies, and the wealthiest and largest city south of Philadelphia. By 1770 it was the fourth largest port in the colonies, after only Boston, New York, and Philadelphia, with a population of 11,000, slightly more than half of that slaves.

Charleston was the hub of the deerskin trade. In fact, deerskin trade was the basis of Charleston's early economy. Trade alliances with the Cherokee and Creek insured a steady supply of deer hides. Between 1699 and 1715, an average of 54,000 deerskins were exported annually to Europe through Charleston. Between 1739 and 1761, the height of the deerskin trade era, an estimated 500,000 to 1,250,000 deer were slaughtered. During the same period, Charleston records show an export of 5,239,350 pounds of deerskins. Deerskins were used in the production of men's fashionable and practical buckskin pantaloons for riding, gloves, and book bindings.

Colonial low-country landowners experimented with cash crops ranging from tea to silk. African slaves brought knowledge of rice cultivation, which plantation owners made into a successful business by 1700. With the help of African slaves from the Caribbean, Eliza Lucas, daughter of plantation owner George Lucas, learned how to raise and use indigo in the Low-Country in 1747. Supported with subsidies from Britain, indigo was a leading export by 1750. Those and naval stores were exported in an extremely profitable shipping industry.

As Charleston grew, so did the community's cultural and social opportunities, especially for the elite merchants and planters. The first theater building in America was built in Charleston in 1736. Benevolent societies were formed by several different ethnic groups. The Charleston Library Society was established in 1748 by some wealthy Charlestonians who wished to keep up with the scientific and philosophical issues of the day. This group also helped establish the College of Charleston in 1770, the oldest college in South Carolina and the oldest municipally supported college in the United States.

Did You Know?

- Fort Sumter's island was constructed with a foundation of over 70,000 tons of granite and other rock. For over a decade contractors from as far away as New York and the Boston area delivered this material by ship and dumped it on a shoal in Charleston Harbor. Fort Sumter National Monument, SC.

- Fort Sumter is a Third System masonry coastal fortification located in Charleston Harbor, South Carolina. The fort is best known as the site upon which the shots initiating the American Civil War were fired at the Battle of Fort Sumter.

Named after General Thomas Sumter Revolutionary War hero, Fort Sumter was built following the War of 1812, as one of a series of fortifications on the southern US coast. Construction began in 1827, and the structure was still unfinished in 1861, when the Civil War began. Seventy thousand tons of granite were imported from New England to build up a sand bar in the entrance to Charleston Harbor, which the site dominates. The fort was a five-sided brick structure, 170 to 190 feet (58 m) long, with walls 5 feet thick, standing 50 feet (15 m) over the low tide mark. It was designed to house 650 men and 135 guns in three tiers of gun emplacements, although it was never filled near its full capacity.

Artist's Rendering—Attack on Fort Sumter

Artist's Rendering—After the Bombardment

Fort Sumter Today – Aerial View

- **First Submarine Attack, Charleston, South Carolina**

As Union ships besieged Charleston in 1863, Confederate military officials turned to a weird, 40-foot-long "torpedo fish," an experimental submarine called the *H. L. Hunley*. The thing sank twice—killing several sailors—during trial runs. Each time it was raised. On February 17, 1864, the *Hunley* torpedoed the USS *Housatonic*, the Union's largest ship. The *Housatonic* sank, and so did the *Hunley*. The sub was recovered in 2001, and a reported 20,000 people turned out for the solemn burial of its eight-man crew.

As for the *Hunley* itself, it's still underwater—only now in a high-tech, refrigerated tank at a Charleston conservation lab, open to the public (877-448-6539; etix.com).

Reconstruction

After the defeat of the Confederacy, Federal forces remained in Charleston during the city's reconstruction. The war had shattered the prosperity of the antebellum city. Freed slaves were faced with poverty and discrimination. Industries slowly brought the city and its inhabitants back to a renewed vitality and growth in population. As the city's commerce improved, Charlestonians also worked to restore their community institutions.

1886 Earthquake

On August 31, 1886, Charleston was nearly destroyed by an earthquake measuring 7.5 on the Richter scale. Major damage was reported as far away as Tybee Island, Georgia (over 60 miles away) and structural damage was reported several hundred miles from Charleston (including central Alabama, central Ohio, eastern Kentucky, southern Virginia, and western West Virginia). It was felt as far away as Boston to the north, Chicago and Milwaukee to the northwest, as far west as New Orleans, as far south as Cuba, and as far east as Bermuda. It damaged 2,000 buildings in Charleston and caused $6 million worth of damage ($133 million [2006 USD]), while in the whole city the buildings were only valued at approximately $24 million ($531 million [2006 USD]).

Michael A Davis

Historic Charleston
(1890s–1900s)

Old Charleston Gate

Oak Avenue at Ashley Hall

Live Oak, Magnolia Cemetery

Huguenot Church

Residences on South Battery East Battery Walkway

Old Cemetery, St. Michael's Cathedral jpg nere — **NOT ON FILE EPROOF LIST**

Charleston College jpg here **– NOT ON FILE PROOF LIST**

Carriage Tour of Old Charleston jpg here – NOT ON FILE PROOF LIST

This, then, is the place and the times in the lives of my ancestors. By 1899, when my father was born, Charleston had recovered physically, if not emotionally, from the destruction of the war and the devastating earthquake a few years earlier. Using concrete to build the majority of their homes and buildings proved fortuitous not only for the city of Charleston but for my family as well.

9

Out of the Shadows

I have lived my entire life without a father, with just a "shadow" of the individual who sired me. Through the years, especially as a child, I kept hoping he would show up. But of course, he never did. Finally, in 2007, as a middle-aged man with nearly grown children of my own, I decided to try and find this man, this enigma, this shadow figure to discover who and what he was.

The mysteries associated with my shadow father began to peel away after I obtained his death certificate. I had started my search by writing letters to the state to obtain his death certificate, because based on his birth date of 1899, he would have been 111 years old at the time. So I figured he had to be deceased.

Several months after my inquiry, the death certificate arrived in the mail, and that's when I learned he died in 1970 in St. Charles, Missouri. This research also turned up the fact that his first wife, Virginia Carrow Hodges Davis, went to Charleston in 1950 and had him legally declared dead. Of course, unknown to her, he was very much alive and living with us, his second family, in Tennessee at this time.

Eventually, I went online with my search and made contact with a cousin, Cynthia Vorhies, via a genealogy website. That's how I learned he was buried in Ravenel, South Carolina. So then I made plans to visit his grave. I flew to Charleston and then drove to the cemetery in Ravenel where he is buried, as recounted elsewhere in this book. I actually visited his gravesite on Good Friday, March 2007.

After that emotional and healing experience, and while still in the Charleston area, I made arrangements to meet with Cynthia in person. She lives in Ladson, South Carolina, about twenty miles from Ravenel. She and her husband, Kirk, have two sons. She is very outgoing. In many ways, she is like a sister to me.

In talking about our Davis ancestors, we discovered our grandfathers were brothers. She was as surprised as I to learn her family was much larger than she ever imagined. She was instrumental in helping me find the rest of my family from Papa's first and third marriages.

With her help, I located Papa's brother, William Nathan "Pete" Davis, and his family, who live in North Charleston. Cynthia got in touch with Pete's daughter Betty, and we met for the first time at the Davis family plot in Whites Church Cemetery. Pete is the brother who took Papa's body back to the family cemetery when he died. They could not believe he had kids in Tennessee. At first they thought I was one of Mardella's grown sons they had seen as a little child at Papa's funeral in 1970. Meeting and talking with Pete is how I learned about Papa's third wife, Mardella, and her children. But I would meet them later.

In June 2008, I went to Port Orange, Florida, and took pictures of the Peninsular Drive house on the St. Johns River, the house Virginia and the kids lived in and built, with the help of her boarders at the time. In talking with a neighbor, Mrs. Miller, I learned that Papa's daughter, my stepsister Nadine Lorraine, had lived there until she died in 2005, and her son, Roger Neil, had inherited this house from his mother.

Mrs. Miller told me Roger was living in San Diego at the time and had just put the house up for sale for $470,000. She gave me his phone number and I called him. At first he thought I was calling to make some financial claim on the house. But when I convinced him I was just there to make contact with my people, he told me there was a chest Papa had built sitting on the back porch of this house, and he wanted me to have it. Roger called his realtor and arranged for him to meet me there so I could get it.

This chest is the only thing left from this period of my father's life. And now I have it. It was only after meeting Amelia later that year that I learned it was the only thing saved from the house that Papa burned down; I will treasure it always.

In November of 2008, I returned to Florida, to Ocala, and that's when I met Amelia Davis Deen for the first time, the only child still living from Papa's first marriage. She shared her memories of Papa with me, which I have reprinted in the section "Amelia's Diary."

She elaborated on Papa's dual personality. Today I think we'd call him bipolar. Amelia told me Papa had the reputation of being the fun-loving "life of the party" with his friends and with his band buddies, the Florida Ramblers. But at home, he would unleash his violent temper on a whim, sadistically beating and abusing them. She witnessed many of these beatings and hated him for it. She still does. She told me she remembers the day he left. He told her he was going to town and promised to take her to the movies to celebrate her eleventh birthday when he returned. He never came back. "It was the best birthday present I ever had," she said.

Finally, in March of 2009, I went to Moberly, Missouri, and met Mardella and her sisters. This meeting turned out very well; they were as anxious to meet us as we were to meet them. It was a great reunion.

And then I met Mardella's children, my siblings. They were skeptical of my purpose, of my motives. They had no idea their father had two other families. I don't know if it was a good or bad thing to tell them the truth, but I finally did it. I think it was hard for them to accept. Mostly they remembered him as a fairly decent, hardworking man whose temper sometimes got the best of him.

Eventually I made them understand I had no ulterior motives, and I have since developed a brother-sister relationship with all of them. I am so glad I finally found them. It was a relief for me to share what I had learned of Papa's extraordinary life with them—the good and the bad. It's infinitely better to know all the truth about someone and then, if you can find it in your heart to forgive and still love them, you have accomplished something. This certainly has been true for me. I hope it is also true for my brothers and sisters.

When I finally returned to Tennessee and began to piece together all this newfound information—pictures and stories of my extended family—I shared it with my brothers Stanley and Clifford. Now it was their turn to be skeptical. I couldn't blame them. It was a lot of information to absorb all at once. As a result of their skepticism, I started digging into our past some more, which is how I found out that Clifford's last name was originally Crabtree and Stanley's was Flores. Talk about weaving a tangled web.

* * *

It has not been easy to discuss all this with my own children. They don't like to talk about it; I think it makes them feel uncomfortable. So I hope they will read this book and understand, as I do, that knowing is always better than not knowing. Once you know something, you can deal with it and learn from it.

Filling the empty spaces in your heart with knowledge is kind of like finding your way out of the woods. You dispel the shapes and the shadows and come out into the light.

And then you can get on with your life.

* * *

Some of the things my Papa did would put him in jail if he did them today. I will never understand how he could walk away from his children—twice. But he did.

I'm so glad I went searching for my father. Retracing his path was painful and disturbing. But in the process, I found so many family members I would never have known if I had not embarked on this painful journey. I am grateful for everything I've learned. I believe I am a better person for it.

I believe it was Maya Angelou who said, "Wouldn't take nothin' for my journey now."

That's exactly how I feel. When God closes one door, He opens another. Whatever life experiences we have will either do us in or make us stronger. To live this life is to endure joy and pain, hardship and blessing. But if we realize it, God is always there, walking—sometimes carrying us—through the trials, the tribulations, the happiness, the joys in this journey of life.

I am grateful for this journey of discovery. It became one of self-discovery as well. Learning who and what my father was, being able to forgive him, and finding these additional family members has been such a blessing. I wouldn't take a million bucks for my brothers and sisters. My heart is full and overflowing with love; it has been an honor getting to know them.

Living in the shadow of my father, wondering who he was, where he was, was difficult. Now his life has been brought out of the shadow for us, his children, to see. Now we can deal with it. We can't go back and change the beginning, but we can make a better ending.

I hope my children, their children, and all who read this will be inspired to discover the dark places, the secrets, the fears in their own lives, to bring them out into the open and face them. Acknowledging and facing the demons is the only way to put them to rest. And that enables you to find peace through acceptance of what is and forgiveness for what was.

And to God we give the Glory.

You can forget about your past,
but your past won't forget about you.
—Author Unknown

Michael A Davis

Me and sister Diane at mama''s Grave 2006

Diane Littler ,Marvelous Myers ,Michael Davis,Florida 2008

Me and kids ,Michael,Krista,Kayla,Davis 2010